T0103589

LEADING IN THE JUNGLE

A Fable of a Chimp's Quest
to Lead like a Gorilla

JOSEPH L. GARCIA

abbott press®

A DIVISION OF WRITER'S DIGEST

Copyright © 2014 Joseph L. Garcia.

All rights reserved. No part of this book may be used or reproduced by any means, graphic, electronic, or mechanical, including photocopying, recording, taping or by any information storage retrieval system without the written permission of the publisher except in the case of brief quotations embodied in critical articles and reviews.

Abbott Press books may be ordered through booksellers or by contacting:

Abbott Press
1663 Liberty Drive
Bloomington, IN 47403
www.abbottpress.com
Phone: 1-866-697-5310

Because of the dynamic nature of the Internet, any web addresses or links contained in this book may have changed since publication and may no longer be valid. The views expressed in this work are solely those of the author and do not necessarily reflect the views of the publisher, and the publisher hereby disclaims any responsibility for them.

Any people depicted in stock imagery provided by Thinkstock are models, and such images are being used for illustrative purposes only. Certain stock imagery © Thinkstock.

ISBN: 978-1-4582-1652-6 (sc)
ISBN: 978-1-4582-1654-0 (hc)
ISBN: 978-1-4582-1653-3 (e)

Library of Congress Control Number: 2014910543

Printed in the United States of America.

Abbott Press rev. date: 06/25/2014

To my beautiful wife Brenda,
my son Jason, and my sister Rosie.

Contents

ACKNOWLEDGEMENTS

To my beautiful and loving wife Brenda for her continued support and inspiration. I value her insightful feedback that has made *Leading in the Jungle* a much better story. To my son Jason, for our playful banter about monkeys over the years that became the origin of the book. His comments and advice were also valuable to the final product. To my good friend Miguel DeJesus, a coworker during Hurricane Katrina recovery operations in New Orleans, Louisiana. We used to do the "great ape" knuckles-to-knuckles handshake well before this book was ever written. Thanks to colleagues and friends, L. C. Williams, Allen Hepner, Patty Bennett, and Anthony Thompson for their review and insight to make the book a much better read. I also thank Citadel Cadets Trevor Brown and Fernando Gonzalez for enhancing the book and to Russ Pace for taking the photo.

Special thanks to Clip Art, Photos.com, and Fotolia for use of their illustrations that greatly enhanced the *Leading in the Jungle* fable by adding life to the characters. For more information, visit their respective websites at www.ClipArt.com, www.Photos.com, and www. us.fotolia.com.

LEADING IN THE JUNGLE
CAST OF CHARACTERS

Taylor: Charles' wife
Charles: chimp executive officer at CHIMP Inc.
Ravae: special assistant to Charles
Cyrus: the board chair at CHIMP Inc.
Gregory: owner of the Modern Jungle Construction Company
Bethany: Dawson's wife
Dawson: gorilla employee injured in a construction accident
Andreas: Gregory's assistant
Gil: branch chief of logistics
Ava: chimp financial officer or CFO
Cliff: chief information officer or CIO
Autumn: chief engineer
Carl: assistant to Cyrus
Hannah: chief of ape resources (AR)
Brayson: personal trainer
Ryan: gorilla union lead
Edna: leader of the elephant herd
Gabe: work yard gorilla employee
Guy: work yard gorilla employee
Grover and Galileo: sons of Dawson and Bethany
Kayla: Gregory's deputy
Nathan: gorilla who developed the fire cistern
Professor Gaylord: headmaster of North Forest Learning Center
Sean: male gorilla student at North Forest Learning Center
Gilda: female gorilla student at North Forest Learning Center

INTRODUCTION:
THE LEADERSHIP JOURNEY

In the fable you are about to read, a chimpanzee named Charles reaches a point common to many of us: burning out from the many challenges and difficulties that come with leadership. His frustrations lead him to wander off aimlessly and eventually end up in North Forest.

Fortunately for Charles, the gorilla community there, led by a wise silverback named Gregory, graciously welcomes the chimpanzee into its midst. There, Charles is able to observe, reflect, and learn from the various gorillas and events that take place around him. As a result, Charles learns more about leadership in a day than he had up to that point in his entire life.

You may ask, "Why use gorillas and chimpanzees for this business fable?"

As leaders, we can sometimes get too close to a situation to process and learn from our own adventures. The colorful animal characters and their jungle habitat give us a visual perspective that allows us to step back and objectively evaluate the experiences that Charles faces in North Forest. In doing so, we can apply valuable lessons to our own leadership journey, one that never ends.

Leading in the Jungle has a story line that is at times humorous as it is moving. Yet make no mistake, the desired outcome is to provide valuable management lessons for both new and experienced leaders.

Periodically, after reading a set of chapters, we will pause to develop what I refer to as GQ. Whereas IQ refers to intelligence quotient and EQ refers to emotional (intelligence) quotient, gorilla quotient or GQ refers to the ability to lead like a seven-hundred-pound gorilla.

After the last chapter, I have posted discussion questions to reinforce your GQ that you have learned throughout the book.

I hope that the leadership journey you will soon embark on is as rewarding as it is entertaining. Let us now begin our jungle excursion.

CHAPTER ONE

It's a Chimp's Life

> It was not that he had a bad job or even disliked going to work really. However lately, things were getting to him more than normal.

"Wake up, sleepyhead. You'll be late for work!"

Charles rolled his eyes and then his body as he sighed to himself. "I am wide awake, Taylor, and I'm not at all sleepy. But anxious to get to work is definitely a stretch."

Wednesday morning had become his least favorite day of the week because it meant the weekly staff meeting. "Hump day" was more like "Chump day" or, to be more exact, "Chimp Day."

His wife, Taylor, was humming to herself as she often did in the morning. Charles slid into his chair for breakfast while glancing at the *South Forest Forum* newspaper.

"Do you have a busy day, dear?" Taylor served his favorite morning meal of bananas and ants.

"No, hon, nothing special," Charles replied.

Why bring her down? he thought.

As Taylor poured him a cup of coconut juice, Charles read the front-page article about his company's new undertaking of enhancing South Forest's communication system. He was the chimp executive officer, or CEO, at CHange and Innovation Makes Progress (CHIMP) Incorporated, and his team was on the hook to complete the important project on time and on budget. The beta phase was almost completed, and they were soon entering the final project phase to stand up the new communication system.

The modern-day venture, labeled "Virtual Vine," would revolutionize the way chimps communicated with each other across longer distances. For close-range conversations (and Taylor had plenty of those around their tree neighborhood), chimps could merely stick their head outside the hut and talk without any problem.

The challenge was conversing with chimps living in trees that were not in their immediate vicinity. For that type of communication, they had to do what their ancestors had been doing for over a hundred years by swinging on a vine across the jungle forest until they landed at the hut of the chimps with whom they needed to communicate.

The South Forest chimp population was growing at a fast rate. Over the years, as chimps mated and had infants, the community was expanding out toward the northern part of the forest. Maintaining a basic communication channel among chimps was only one of numerous challenges they would face in the future. The chimp society needed improved infrastructure—schools, hospitals, recreation centers, and so on—to keep up with their needs.

Recent studies had also shown that the chimp community was getting older. For some of the more mature chimps, clinging on a vine sixty feet in the air was not as easy as it used to be. There were also chimps with special needs that prevented them from the physical activity necessary with chimp-to-chimp, long-range communication.

With Virtual Vine, instead of physically swinging on a vine, CHIMP Inc. had proposed using the vine itself as a means to communicate remotely. The engineers at the company had discovered that, by stretching the vine extremely tight and reinforcing with dry mud around it for insulation from the elements, Virtual Vine could connect every tree and hut.

The vine system was first distributed across the highest trees. Next, the vines were dropped down the hollow part of the main trees and into each hut connected via a coconut shell. The shell would serve as a device to speak and listen across the entire South Forest. As part of the pilot phase, Charles had even installed one of the new devices into his hut so he could occasionally speak to Taylor from his office.

"It seems to me you will be having a lot of busy days from now on, from what I can read."

Charles knew better than try to deceive Taylor. She was always the smarter of the two, and the trouble was that both of them knew it. Taylor was probably more ably suited then he was to be leading the latest CHIMP Inc. project.

They had met while students at South Forest College. She was popular and earned top grades. He, on the other hand, was a star fullback and captain of the football team. Charles seemed to have a knack of leading others toward meeting whatever mission was in front of them. Whether winning football games on the field or successfully completing projects, the chimp community grew to respect him and rely on his leadership ability.

Soon, Charles had descended from their hut in the large tree and started walking on the trail leading to his office. It was not that he had a bad job or even disliked going to work really. However lately, things were getting to him more than normal. And staff meetings! It was literally a three-ring circus, and he was the announcer, the chimp on the high wire, and the clown with the big shoes and red nose all rolled into one!

As he stepped into the main CHIMP Inc. building, his assistant Ravae greeted him and handed him the staff meeting agenda and a few issues papers.

"They're all gathered, sir. Cyrus wants to see you right away after your staff meeting to discuss this morning's newspaper article and the budget. Do you need anything else?"

"No thanks. I'll be fine."

Thank goodness for Ravae, he thought. He could always count on his special assistant to be organized and supportive amid all the chaos. He made a mental note to tell her as much.

With a deep breath, Charles opened the door to the conference room. "Let the mayhem begin," he muttered to himself.

CHAPTER TWO

◆

Gregory, The Alpha Ape

> Gregory was the founder and owner of the Modern Jungle Construction Company, North Forest's largest firm. He employed nearly three hundred gorillas in construction, renovation, and repairs.

"I understand, Bethany." Gregory took his mammoth hands and patted his visitor on her much smaller ones to demonstrate his genuine concern. "Let me see what I can do, and I promise to get back with you just as soon as I can."

Bethany was the wife of Dawson, one of Gregory's subordinates. Dawson had injured himself in a construction accident a few months earlier. Like so many of the employee spouses, Gregory knew Bethany personally, along with their young primates, Grover and Galileo. He encouraged family members to participate in the regular company picnics or sporting events. Gregory was there when the infant Grover had fallen from a tree and landed on his head. Gregory picked him up and handed him to Bethany, who came scrambling toward the tree in a panic.

Bethany was concerned because Dawson had missed so much work that he might be laid off or even dismissed.

"Thank you, Gregory. I knew I could count on you." Bethany quietly left with her pride and dignity intact.

"Andreas, come in here, please."

His young assistant was at Gregory's desk within seconds with his memo pad and pencil in hand to capture his boss' request. He was part of the recent graduate intern program that Gregory had started a few years earlier at the local college.

"See Hannah from AR [ape resources] and ask her to pull the file on Dawson's case and set up a meeting with me this afternoon. I want to know what options we have before making a final decision on Dawson's work status."

"You got it, boss."

And just as quickly as he entered, Andreas was off to make it happen.

Gregory was the founder and owner of the Modern Jungle Construction Company, North Forest's largest firm. He employed nearly three hundred gorillas in construction, renovation, and repairs. In addition to the frontline workforce, his company employed back office staff personnel, including accounting, AR, and procurement.

Extremely popular, Gregory had often been encouraged to run for public office. The current mayor even teased him that he would never stand a chance if Gregory threw his hat in the ring. Gregory felt satisfied in his current business role, and he often assisted the community through charitable contributions or other means of influence.

Satisfied that he completed all the necessary tasks and paperwork for the morning, Gregory had some time before his scheduled workout with his personal trainer. He decided to do what he actually enjoyed the best, getting out and connecting with his employees, customers, and business partners.

CHAPTER THREE

Climbing the Corporate Tree

> The younger apes had coined a new term just for Gil,
> "Cool School," someone who was old fashioned in many
> ways but also someone they respected and liked.

G regory leisurely moved through the large business compound, greeting employees and stopping to chat with them for a few minutes. He decided to visit Gil, the branch chief in charge of logistics.

Gil had actually been with Modern Jungle Construction Company as long as Gregory had, about twenty years. Gil started in the backbreaking job of big tree removal in order to clear the land for construction of schools, hospitals, and office building as new businesses and local government began to grow. Gil was extremely loyal to Gregory, who counted on him to coordinate all the supplies and building materials necessary to make the many construction and maintenance projects successful.

He had a reputation of being a tough taskmaster, but virtually all the younger apes petitioned to work in Gil's logistics area. They enjoyed the outdoor work and the chance to hear his stories and experiences from the early days of the firm. Gil was the only branch chief that actually had kept his office in the tree. Others worked in an office throughout the complex. The younger apes had coined a new term just for Gil, "Cool School," someone who was old fashioned in many ways but also someone they respected and liked.

Gregory climbed up to Gil's office in the top of the branch and greeted his old friend. "Any ape home?"

Gil's desk faced away from the front entrance, but recognizing Gregory's voice, he replied without looking up, "Just us baboons."

He was always fond to see his long-standing comrade, and he extended his right paw outward as Gregory did the same until the two lightly touched knuckles.

"How about a cup of coconut juice?" Gil asked as Gregory sat down in the chair next to Gil's desk.

"No thanks. I'm working out in a few minutes, and I don't like anything in my stomach. Brayson wants me to do more cardio after strength training. He thinks I'm gaining weight."

Gil laughed. "You're still the alpha ape in the jungle, my friend! Even the young ones give you plenty of space when you come around."

"Maybe so. But Brayson is a certified trainer, so I will let him do his job."

"Speaking of someone doing his job, I met with Ryan yesterday about union concerns. He is worried about what is going to happen to Dawson. Ryan reminds me that, in his role as steward, his job is to protect the rights of all the apes in the union."

After a few moments, Gregory said slowly, "It shouldn't matter if Dawson belongs to the union or not. He was hurt on the job, and I have scheduled a meeting later today with Hannah to look at all our options."

Gil knew he was bringing up a delicate subject, the union. Gregory had assigned him to be the company's management liaison on union issues years ago. Gregory had explained that Gil could relate to the union members who were primarily from the construction and logistics workforce.

In some cases, Gregory felt that Ryan and the union stewards were focused too much on which ape was a dues-paying member of the United Union of Tree Removers, Construction Workers, and Logisticians.

"Okay, Gil, I better get moving before Brayson makes me run an extra mile on the treadmill for being late."

"He wouldn't dare do that to the boss."

"Actually, he would."

◆

Chapter Four

Chaos in the Conference Room

> Instead of collectively reaching a sound and logical business
> decision, they were letting emotions and ego get in the
> way. Frankly, Charles was getting tired of the pattern.

"No way, no how, Cliff. I'll be a monkey's aunt before you get your unfunded request." Ava, the chimp financial officer (CFO), was drawing the line in the sand even quicker than normal. "You should have submitted your budget requirement on time like everybody else."

Cliff, the chimp information officer (CIO), was swinging at the top of the conference room vine while looking down at Ava. "Give me a break, Ava. You and I have talked about the extra money that we might need based on the beta test. We never planned for a second layer of mud for all of the vines. The engineers are saying we will need that second layer for clarity of the conversations over the longer distances. If you got a problem with anyone, it ought to be Autumn. She's the chief engineer on the project, not me."

"Don't look at me." Autumn retorted. "I was the one who said from the beginning that a second coat of mud was going to be the best approach. You guys chose to ignore my recommendation, and now you're trying to throw me under the rhino."

Charles raised both arms and sought to gain control of the situation. "Please, let's keep our emotions in check. Cliff, come on down. Let's try to talk this problem through and come up with a solution."

As Cliff scampered down, some of the chimps in the room tried unsuccessfully to conceal their giggles.

"Charles, we sat here a month ago, and I reminded everyone that any budget changes needed to be put on paper, coordinated, and then cleared by the board. I am just trying to protect you. After all, you are going to need to convince Cyrus that we need the additional funds. And we all know he protects the company's assets like a mother lioness does her cubs from hyenas."

Charles sat silently, taking in the scene around him. Each of these CHIMP Inc. executives had risen up the corporate tree based primarily on their technical skills. Ava, an excellent accountant, could balance the books and be prepared for an audit at any time. Charles relied on her for financial advice, and more often than not, Ava was always on the money, so to speak.

Cliff, although prone to occasional theatrics, was very innovative and forward thinking. To his credit, he proposed the idea for Virtual Vine over a year ago. He took a lot of heat because it sounded preposterous at the time. Cliff stood his ground and championed the idea when others might have backed down. Autumn, the chief engineer, was probably the best thinker in the group. She had to take Cliff's idea and then figure out a way to develop the project plan to bring it to fruition. Each of these senior chimps was highly intelligent.

Intellect is not the problem, Charles thought.

The challenge was that they tended to look at things from only their point of view, and as a result, they would inevitably expect Charles to solve all the problems. Instead of collectively reaching a sound and logical business decision, they were letting emotions and ego get in the way. Frankly, Charles was getting tired of the pattern.

"Autumn, are you sure that the second mud layer is absolutely necessary? Could something else be distorting the long-range communication, like the vines themselves?"

"No, Charles, I already thought of that. I had my engineers run a diagnostic analysis in the lab from ant to zebra. The vines work fine, the coconut devices are not the problem, and it has nothing to do with the distance itself. One coat of mud covering is just porous enough that the voice communication literally leaks through small cracks. The second mud application will seal up those tiny holes completely. And that is what I recommended early on."

"Ava, do we have a firm estimate on what the second mud layer will cost? I need good numbers before I go back to Cyrus and the rest of the board."

"My cost chimps are cranking through the calculations as we speak. I can tell you that it may put us over budget for the project."

"Ava, wait a minute." Autumn held her index finger in the air. "While that part is true for the second mud application, we have also been cost efficient in other areas. Our Virtual Vine plan was based on eight hundred coconuts shipped in from our supplier. We now realize that the actual device only requires half of a coconut. We can merely cut a coconut in half and use it for two devices, not just one. That will save us some supply money along with a few other cost initiatives we've taken."

Some of the other chimps at the table were soon nodding their heads in agreement. It looked like they had perhaps made a breakthrough.

"Okay, I want Autumn and Cliff to get together to modify their plan and get it to Ava so her cost chimps can price out the whole effort. I really need it within a day or two. I can't keep putting off Cyrus forever."

At that point, Charles adjourned the session. He checked in with Ravae before heading over for his meeting with Cyrus.

"Your meeting with Cyrus is in thirty minutes. I wanted to make sure you had some time to decompress after your staff meeting." Ravae gave him a half grin that Charles understood that she knew what went on at a typical gathering of his executive chimps. "I also talked to Carl to get a little intelligence before your meeting."

Carl was a special assistant to Cyrus but had started in the front office under Ravae's tutelage. They were still close.

"Carl said that, as far as the article today, Cyrus had one major concern. There was an indication that any cost overruns on the project would pass on to the chimpanzee customer community. He definitely does not want that kind of negative publicity. Of course, that ties to his request to go over the numbers with you to see the projected budget-to-actuals for the remainder of the year.

"While you were in your staff meeting, I did some calculations as best I could. Even if the Virtual Vine project goes slightly over budget, your efforts to keep costs down throughout CHIMP Inc. puts us in a good position to actually exceed our overall net revenue targets. I have the numbers in case you need to go over any of the specifics with Cyrus."

"Wow! Thanks, Ravae. This is excellent work all around. I want to thank you for all that you do for me and the company."

"Just doing my job, Chief. Now why don't you relax in your office for a few minutes and just unwind. Or go through some of this information. I will try to keep away any visitors in the meantime."

"Thank you again." Charles closed the door behind him as he slouched in his chair.

He took Ravae's counsel and just closed his eyes for a few moments. He would look at her calculations in a few minutes, but he trusted her work.

"Charles, you better get going. Your meeting is in five minutes."

He must have dozed off because he heard her knocking on the door getting louder with each thump.

"I'm coming, Ravae."

I must really be worn out, Charles thought. *I never fell asleep in a meeting or certainly in my office.*

It was a good thing that Ravae had given him enough lead time to compose himself before the short walk to Cyrus' office.

"Come in, Charles. Come on in." Cyrus happened to be in the reception area getting a second cup of coconut juice. "I was just telling Carl here that you should always expect an article in the *Forum* to look for a negative spin of some kind. Overall, I thought it was a favorable article. Let's sit down so I can draft an editorial response to set the record straight on the project overruns."

The board chair chimp put his long arm around Charles' neck as he closed the door behind him. "Actually, Charles, I'm more concerned about our projected end-of-year numbers. The board knows you are doing a great job, but our major investors get a little skittish."

"Cyrus, I think we'll be okay." Charles pulled the documents that Ravae had prepared for him.

After several hours and two pots of coconut juice later, Cyrus was convinced enough to show Charles out of his office while giving him a mixed message. "I have complete confidence in your ability, Charles. Just don't get eaten by a lion. CHIMP Inc. would be in real trouble without you."

Charles found himself thinking about what Cyrus told him as he began to walk on the trail at the edge of the complex, in no hurry to get back to his office.

Was that a compliment Cyrus had given me? Or was it actually something not meant as positive at all? As Charles kept walking, he found himself thinking about lots of things. *Am I a successful leader if my company would fall apart without me? Am I feeling a bit grumpy and tired lately because I took too much on myself? Am I enabling my staff or actually underdeveloping them? Is there a lion in the vicinity that I did not know about?*

He shrugged off the last notion as silly of course, but his mind continued to churn out some deep and even conflicting thoughts. Charles realized that, by walking on the trail at this time of the day, it was his first time alone to himself in who knew how long. It felt refreshing, both physically and mentally.

Soon, Charles realized something else. He was so lost in his thoughts that he had walked for several hours. He was off the trail and at the far edge of South Forest. Charles looked around and saw the sun setting behind the large trees that served as a natural border along South Forest from North Forest. It would be too dark to walk the long distance back to his office. He decided to spend the night on top of the high tree line. After all, maybe there were lions or other predators that would be out soon for a night hunt.

Fortunately, he remembered that Autumn had proposed installing the Virtual Vine lines to the end of South Forest boundary, something about potential future development and just putting them in now instead of later. Charles found a coconut, scampered up the tree, and located a set of the Virtual Vine.

When all the vine devices were installed in each chimp household, it would take a unique combination to reach a particular hut. The outer shell of the coconut would contain three vertical holes with wooden pegs installed at the left end of each hole. Each of the vertical holes contained five separate grooves that the peg could be moved to the right to fit. A combination of two-four-five meant second peg under the first hole, fourth peg under the second hole, and fifth peg under the third hole. Once the combination was set, the caller could merely start speaking into the hollow part of the coconut, and the receiver would hear the voice on the other end and do the same.

This last phase of installing the coconut devices was set to begin in a few weeks. That meant that the current Virtual Vine system was wide open and accessible to only a select group of pilot users, Charles and his wife Taylor, Cliff, and Autumn.

Because he was the CEO, the combination for Charles was one-one-one. In short order, he had made a crude connection and configured the basic vine combination to connect with Taylor.

"Charles, is that you?"

"Yes, hon, it's me."

"Where are you? Ravae dropped by after work to see if you had gone home. She knew you were with Cyrus for a long while, but they told her that you had left earlier. Are you okay?"

For a moment, Charles felt guilty for deciding to spend the night on this side of the forest. After all, he could stay on top of the tree line and avoid the low ground where most of the predators hunted. He just needed some quiet time to think things through a bit more.

"Yes, hon, I am fine. Honest. I am here on the border of South Forest and North Forest. I just wanted to test the full range of the Virtual Vine to see if it worked from one side to the next. Our recent tests have been limited in distance." Charles felt bad for stretching the truth. "So just tell Ravae that I am going to do a physical check on this side of the forest so I will be out tomorrow. There is no need to send anybody out here. I will be fine."

By the silence on the other end of the line, Charles knew that Taylor felt there was more to it than that. She decided not to ask Charles any more questions. If she knew the truth, it would be hard to cover for her husband.

"Okay, dear. Just be careful. That part of the forest is not developed and can get a bit dangerous at night."

"You mean like lions on the prowl?"

"No, dear, not in particular. What makes you bring up lions? Did you see any?"

"No, hon, I am just kidding. I love you, and I will see you late tomorrow afternoon. I promise."

He disconnected the line and went to sleep.

DEVELOPING YOUR
GORILLA QUOTIENT (GQ):
FIRST REFLECTION

An effective leader moves at a deliberate pace

We immediately notice the difference in the stress levels between Charles, the CEO of CHIMP Inc., and Gregory, the founder and owner of Modern Jungle Construction Company. The chimpanzee had reached the point of not wanting to even get out of bed and face his leadership responsibilities. On the other hand, the gorilla appeared composed and in control as the boss of a larger organization. A gorilla moves slowly compared to a chimpanzee. In the same manner, a leader needs to move deliberatively, guided by his or her principles to get through the strains of leadership.

The importance of demonstrating compassion

As a leader progresses through the ranks, he or she begins to work his or her way up the ladder by virtue of job performance, experience, education, or individual awards, that is, a record of accomplishment. Along the way, he or she obtains more authority and power. How you use that newfound influence is critically important to continued success.

In Gregory's case, our first exposure to his leadership style is not one of pounding of his chest to demonstrate that he is the alpha ape. Everybody knows that, he does not need to remind those around him. Instead, we see Gregory's genuine compassion demonstrated to the spouse of an injured worker, who was concerned about how the family would make ends meet.

In *Resonant Leadership*, Boyatzis and McKee note, "Compassion is empathy and caring in action."[1]

Let me share with you an example of how another leader demonstrated compassion to my son Jason and me. Jason was returning on personal leave from England, where he was stationed in the Air Force. While in transit, his grandmother unfortunately passed away. As a result, we needed to travel to the funeral in Arizona and still get him back to England by his leave's end. I was assigned at the Pentagon in Washington DC at the time.

Because we were both on active duty, one cost-savings option was to fly space available, or "Space A," on military aircraft. Space A travel is a nice benefit for military members but often requires a bit of luck and lots of patience compared to commercial air travel.

We drove to a nearby military installation, signed up for Space A, and then began the waiting game. Then all of a sudden, a flight appeared on the monitor that was going exactly where we needed to go. The transportation crew, however, told us there might be good news and bad news.

The good news was that there was indeed a military mission with open seats to accommodate both of us. The bad news was that there was a general on board, who, although not part of the official crew, had hoped to take advantage of the situation and fly the plane himself. He was a rated Air Force pilot so it would give him a rare opportunity to fly and keep his flight skills current. The problem was that, under safety regulations, no Space A passengers were allowed on board. Jason and I felt deflated as it appeared our good fortune was slipping away.

After a while, one of the sergeants relayed to us that, when the general heard we were traveling on emergency leave orders, he turned down the rare opportunity to fly the plane. We soon boarded in the back of the large cargo aircraft, full of equipment. Shortly before takeoff, the general visited us to pass on his condolences and to see if we needed anything.

---

[1] Richard Boyatzis and Annie McKee, *Resonant Leadership: Renewing Yourself and Connecting with Others Through Mindfulness, Hope, and Compassion* (Boston: Harvard Business School, 2005), 178–179.

When we finally arrived at our destination, we noticed a white staff car with a silver star displayed on the front fender, typical protocol for a general. As Jason and I exited the plane (we had no one waiting for us), the general suddenly picked up our baggage and walked it over to his waiting staff car. He told the surprised driver to take us over to the terminal so we could continue with our travels expeditiously. The general instead, without fanfare, walked to the terminal.

In the military, a general is treated with utmost respect that is deserving of the person achieving such rank. He or she is also given plenty of space, in the manner someone would if encountering a large gorilla in the jungle. In this case, the general would have been acting within his right to keep his flying skills current as part of his important position and rank. Instead, his willingness to give up a rare chance to fly, visit us in the back of the plane crowded with equipment, personally carry our baggage, and give up his waiting staff car demonstrated his humility, unselfishness, and real concern for two fellow airmen in need. I will never forget this true leader's compassion and humility.

The need to check your instruments

The higher a leader advances in an organization, he or she can become isolated from the events occurring on a daily basis at the working level. General Colin Powell once observed, "Whenever I took command of a unit, I announced early on that my bias was toward the guys in the field. I took their word as ground truth."[2] He went on to state, "Over my long years of experience, the line was right about 70 percent of the time."[3]

We note that Gregory, after completing his own tasks, managed by wandering the complex, and on this occasion, he took the time to visit Gil, one of his branch chiefs. During the encounter, he obtained valuable information about union negotiations that he might not have received otherwise.

---

[2] Colin Powell, *It Worked For Me: In Life and Leadership* (New York: Harper Collins, 2012), 93.

[3] Ibid., 94.

The following story demonstrates the importance of getting out from behind your desk and following up to ensure what you think is happening on your organizational radar is actually occurring.

My wife Brenda and I served two years on the Retiree Appreciation Days Committee for our installation. At the request of the commander, I was the chairman who led a group of volunteers who sought to show our appreciation and respect for military retirees living near the base. As the big day drew near, we had arranged to get out one last bit of publicity by me appearing on a popular morning show at one of the local television stations.

Shortly after Brenda and I arrived at the station, the weatherman (and a local celebrity in his own right) came in from outside and entered the studio. He looked at us with a sheepish grin and said, "Just checking the weather myself. You can't always trust the gadgets in front of you."

His point hit home. Leaders should confirm reality themselves.

CHAPTER FIVE

Gorilla Meets Chimp

> The head of the Modern Jungle Construction Company,
> an ape large in stature, both in physique and in
> prominence, was walking with a chimpanzee.

Charles woke up early and a bit stiff. He missed his own bed, but he felt a sense of vigor as he climbed down from the tall tree. After foraging for a quick breakfast of leaves and a few insects, he began to walk toward North Forest.

He knew a gorilla community was in this part of the jungle, but he did not feel afraid. Gorillas and chimpanzees were not natural enemies. Long ago, they had settled in their respective communities and essentially left each other alone. Charles, however, wanted to keep walking to free his mind and contemplate his own direction.

No marker of any kind indicated that he had crossed into North Forest, but he instinctively knew he was clearly in gorilla territory. There were different smells, sounds, and sights compared to South Forest. It was not better or worse necessarily. It was just different.

After a short while, he found a pool to refresh himself. As he dipped down for a drink, he noticed a reflection of a very large ape in the pond. Charles did not panic or show fear. He continued to slowly drink the cool water while eyeing the gorilla's reflection to see if he suddenly moved.

"Good morning, friend. Did you sleep well?"

Charles looked up and up before looking into the eyes of a massive gorilla. He had never been this close up to one before, only seeing them rarely on occasion but always from a distance.

"I did. But how did you know I had been sleeping?"

"I sometimes get up early in the morning and come out this far to spend time with nature. It always refreshes me. You were still sleeping when I arrived, but you woke up shortly after I got here. How were those grasshoppers? I never tasted any before."

"Not as good as the bananas and ants my wife makes me, but it had to do today. I miss my morning coconut juice though."

The giant ape laughed. "I can't promise any ants, but I can get you a cup of coconut juice. Come on. Follow me back to the village. My name is Gregory."

"Charles. Pleasure to meet you."

As Charles strode next to Gregory, he could not help but notice how huge and strong his walking companion was. The great ape moved leisurely through the trail toward the gorilla community. Charles could actually feel the ground beneath him move each time Gregory put one massive paw in front of the other. Gregory did not speak, but somehow it was not an awkward silence.

Charles began noticing other gorillas moving about as they apparently entered into the outskirts of the village. A few of the primates stopped to marvel at the sight in front of them. The head of Modern Jungle Construction Company, an ape large in stature, both in physique and in prominence, was walking with a chimpanzee.

"You don't strike me as someone who is easily intimidated, Charles, but rest assured that you are safe here."

"Thanks, Gregory. If I were one of them, I would probably be staring too. I don't sense any harm though."

"That's good. Come on. We're almost to my office."

CHAPTER SIX

Andreas, the Amiable Ape Assistant

> "I actually want to see new sights and do different things.
> My dad said I always had a restless side to me."

The young assistant turned to greet his boss when he noticed the chimpanzee walking in front of Gregory through the door. "Good morning, sir. I've got a fresh pot of coconut juice going."

"Andreas, I want you to meet Charles. He is our guest, so please do whatever it takes to make him feel at home."

"Absolutely, boss. Charles, it is a pleasure to meet you. Welcome to North Forest."

"Charles could use some of your famous coconut juice, Andreas. Please pour him a cup. There are a couple of construction permits I need to sign right away." Gregory excused himself while he went inside his office.

Andreas opened the storage cabinet and brought out a new cup with the Mighty Jungle logo on it.

As he poured the juice, he said, "Charles, please have a seat in the reception area." He handed Charles the delightful brew.

Charles asked, "What is it that Gregory does again? Judging by the way the other gorillas looked at him, this nice office, and such a sharp assistant as you, he must be an important ape."

"Thank you for the compliment. You are too kind. Actually, it is my privilege to be working for Gregory. He is a great boss. In fact, he is the founder and owner of Mighty Jungle Construction Company." Andreas leaned over to whisper, "Or as my college buddies are fond to say, MJC2. Gregory literally made North Forest what it is today. When he and another gorilla named Gil first arrived, the community was no different from any other gorilla group. Gregory thought of actually tearing down trees so they could build up the town. It was a radical idea at the time. Not many apes went along at first, but Gil helped to convince them to give Gregory a chance."

Charles inquired, "So is Gil the co-owner of MJC2?"

"You know, Charles, that is a good question. The answer is no, although Gil worked side by side Gregory in the early days before Gregory could hire additional help. Gil did not want any part of the politics involved to get the business going. He just enjoyed being in the fresh air and building things."

"I see." Charles nodded. "This Gil gorilla sounds like an interesting ape. I would like to meet him if that is possible."

"Of course, I don't see why not. I am not sure what Gregory plans to do with you today, but he should be out of his office soon, and I can ask him."

"Tell me more about Gregory. You mentioned that he and Gil came to North Forest around the same time. Did they know each other before, and where did they come from?"

"They came from different communities from what I understand. They both do not talk much about their past before arriving to North Forest. There are some interesting stories about both of them. It is hard to know what is legend and what is real."

Deciding not to pry further, Charles turned the conversation in a new direction. "What about you, Andreas? Are you from here originally?"

"Yes, sir, born and raised here. Most of the gorillas are. Very few are like Gregory and Gil who came over as newcomers."

"So you like it here?" Charles moved to the front window that overlooked the heart of North Forest.

"I do, Charles, but I actually want to see new sights and do different things. My dad said I always had a restless side to me."

Charles thought to himself, *New sights? What do you call this?*

All in front of him were things Charles had never even imagined. They figured out how to use the land itself as a foundation upon which to build structures upon other structures. It was an ingenious idea. Judging by the size of some of the buildings, Charles could only fathom what type of ape power went into the construction projects.

Charles turned his attention back to the young ape. "Are you going to school, or do you work here full time as Gregory's assistant?"

"Gregory started a recent graduate intern program, and I was one of the first hired by Mighty Jungle. I started in AR ... uh, ape resources ... but Gregory needed someone to help in the front office so I volunteered. Hannah was not too happy, but Gregory selected a student about to graduate and backfilled me."

Just then, Gregory's office door opened. "Charles, I apologize for leaving you for so long. I am not as smart as Andreas is here, so I need to concentrate in going over the construction permits and the corresponding building orders. We had an accident awhile back that I feel can be traced back to lack of attention on my part. Ever since then, I go over every sentence before I sign the final papers."

"Boss, you are too hard on yourself. The investigation blamed faulty equipment for the accident."

Gregory, towering above the younger ape, looked down at him. He lowered his voice. "Andreas, I am the one with the final signature. As far as I am concerned, I am accountable for Dawson's accident, not some piece of equipment."

The assistant looked down, and Charles could barely make out the "Yes, sir" that Andreas humbly offered to Gregory.

Sensing a need to change the mood, Gregory clapped his two gigantic paws together. "Come, Charles. Let me show you around the complex. Let us leave young Andreas to continue doing great things. Like ensuring his former boss Hannah comes see me after lunch."

"You got it, boss. It was nice visiting with you, Charles. Enjoy your stay."

Seems the young ape has a resiliency to bounce back quickly, Charles thought as he and Gregory stepped through the front door.

CHAPTER SEVEN

◆

The Splendor of North Forest

> "The compound is so well laid out," Charles
> said. "There is a balance and symmetry to it
> that does not exist in my community."

G regory led Charles about two hundred yards to the center of the compound and allowed his visitor to take in the panorama before saying anything. He could see the chimpanzee shaking his head slightly as he looked all around him.

Charles muttered, "Fantastic. Simply fantastic."

Gregory added context to what Charles was seeing with his wide-open eyes. "To our north is the education complex, the Learning Center," Gregory stated proudly. "There are schools for the youngest apes all the way to our North Forest College." Gregory turned around. "To our south is the production and logistics area. Just to the left is my office, where we just came from."

Turning to his right, Gregory pointed to public buildings that included the mayor's office, a hospital, a public library, a fitness center, and a park with a walking trail. "I spend a lot of time on that side." Gregory laughed. "Fortunately, not in the hospital ... but in the mayor's office where the construction permits are processed. Of course, when the mayor sees me, he wants to talk politics or seek nominations for one advisory board or the other. I also work out at the gym several days a week." Turning around one last time, Gregory saved the best for last. "There is my favorite part of our community."

Charles had not noticed it before, but in front of him was a large amphitheater that could seat hundreds.

"We use that venue to hold town meetings, and the North Forest Arts Society sponsors weekly plays and concerts. During election time, there are public debates held there too."

"The compound is so well laid out," Charles said. "There is a balance and symmetry to it that does not exist in my community."

"Charles, I been meaning to ask you. What exactly do you do for a living? You carry yourself with confidence yet humility. You have an inquisitive nature, a good thing."

Charles looked down for a moment. "I work at CHIMP Inc., which stands for CHange and Innovation Makes Progress. Our company tries to enhance our community's quality of life by coming up with new ideas. Right now, we are almost ready to roll out a new communication system that will allow conversations over long distances."

"We could certainly use an idea like that. I get worn out from walking from my office to the permit office every day to see if my construction warrants are signed. I get the feeling you are being modest about your work with CHIMP Inc. Not that it matters to me, but what is your position?"

Charles again looked downward before replying, "I am the chimp executive officer or CEO for short."

"Very impressive, Charles, and I am not surprised."

"Gregory, you know what I find impressive?" Charles pointed to the five-story structure in the education complex. "That. Can we take a closer look? I want to see how it is built and reinforced to not collapse."

"Of course, but I am sure an innovative chimp ... uh, sorry ... CEO like yourself will not be impressed once you see it from the inside. It is all about heavy manual work. Nothing more."

When Gregory began walking away from the impressive construction, Charles inquired, "Where are we going? I thought we were going inside the building."

"Patience, my friend. Patience."

Charles, confused and disappointed, decided to remain quiet and see where Gregory was taking them. "Easy, chimpie," Charles told himself. "You're beginning to act like Cliff. Before you know it, you will be swinging through the trees and complaining to Gregory."

Gregory looked down at the top of Charles' head. "Did I say something funny?"

Apparently, Charles must have chuckled to himself to cause Gregory's question. "No, I was just clearing my throat."

Soon, they were walking back toward the vicinity of Gregory's office, which they were now passing to their left. They continued until they reached a large open area surrounded by the jungle's tall trees. Gregory motioned his giant head for Charles to follow him up a tree with an office on top.

"Any ape home?"

"No, just us baboons."

Gregory, feeling embarrassed, looked back at Charles, who was entering the office door. If Gil's remark offended the chimpanzee, he did not seem to show it. Clearing his throat loudly, Gregory got Gil's attention, who initially was startled by the sight of a chimpanzee in his office, a first for sure.

"Gil, I would like you to meet Charles. Charles, this is Gil, our branch chief of logistics."

"Gr ... Gr ... Greetings," was all Gil could muster.

"Pleasure to meet you, Gil," Charles answered smartly.

Chimps one and gorillas zero, Gregory thought inwardly.

"Gil, our visitor here is from South Forest. Charles is the chimp executive officer of a company there. I have been showing him around the compound, and he was very impressed with the buildings, especially the school with its five stories. Before going inside the facility, I think it would help for him to see how the actual floors are made, the key to the whole assembly. Show him the tree-cutting demo, and then we can go outside to see one actually being produced."

Regaining his composure, Gil stepped over to a table in the corner of the office and motioned Charles to get close. Gregory stayed back to allow his visitor Gil's complete attention. Gil pulled a small tree branch from a box on the table. It had been stripped of any limbs.

"Charles, imagine that this is a large fallen tree. The demo is with a branch, but the concept is the same with any size tree, even the tallest ones that we need to use."

"Got it," Charles said.

Gil brought out two other branches, separated them, and laid the one branch he had been holding between them so it was off the ground. "As you can see, all the limbs, every single one, are cut off from the tree. We have apprentice gorillas that start in that capacity."

Reaching into another box, Gil pulled out a branch of the same size, but it was completely bare of any bark. "Once the limbs are off, another crew takes a flat rock and gets under the bark to strip it again as you can see. Removing the bark keeps the insects out of the newly constructed buildings. When the tree is nothing but core wood, a specialist draws a straight line right down the middle, from one end to the other. Then the tree is turned over, and another straight line is drawn. There are ways to keep the line straight, but you get the point.

"Next, another set of apes chisels away on the line with flat rocks that have been flattened by hitting them with other rocks. We try to cut about a foot into the tree. Once that is done on one side, we repeat on the other side. This is probably the hardest part of all, especially on your back. Right, Gregory?"

"Oh, yes. Absolutely." Gregory spoke up. Gil's attempt to keep him engaged caught him a bit off guard.

Gil said, "You can probably figure out the rest. Two teams of gorillas line up alongside opposite sides of the tree. They begin to pull the tree toward them, and eventually because of the precision cuts, the tree splits in the middle. It is hard work, but in the end, we have two logs ready to be used instead of just one."

Charles thought, *Just like our coconut.*

"Gil, this has been very helpful. Just one more question. How do you get the trees down in the first place?"

"I am going to let Gregory take that one. He is the brains of the outfit. My crew and I are the muscle part. Although I have to say, these younger apes have nothing on Gregory when it comes to sheer strength."

Gregory stepped closer to the two and noted while patting his stomach, "I don't know, Gil. I put on a few pounds over the years. After a workout with Dawson, I feel like one tired, old ape."

"Don't listen to him, Charles. He is still the alpha ape in North Forest."

Eager to get the subject off himself, Gregory turned to Charles. "Again, my friend, you demonstrate why the chimpanzees are considered to be the most intellectual of the ape family. When Gil and I started ... uh ... let's say a few years back ... after a heavy rain, we would climb up and put large rocks in branches on one side of the tree. Over time, it begins to pull up the roots. Then we would assemble the strongest apes to push from one side until it falls over. Fun stuff, right, Gil? As I told you when I first met you, Charles, I sometimes get up early in the morning and—"

Charles smiled. "And spend time with nature. It refreshes you."

Gregory grinned in return. "You have a good memory, my friend, just like an elephant. Which leads me perfectly to the rest of the story. One morning, I had gone for a long walk to the opposite side of the jungle where I first met you. As you know, I can sit pretty quietly where others around me do not even know I am there."

Charles laughed. "I'll say! How does a six hundred-pound gorilla turn invisible?"

Gil leaned over. "Try seven hundred pounds."

Gregory kept speaking. "Well anyway, I am enjoying the rising sun and the awakening of the day when I noticed a herd of elephants far off to the side of me. Charles, do you know the alpha elephant can weigh twenty times my heaviness and be almost twice as tall?"

CHAPTER EIGHT

◆

Elephants in the Neighborhood

> "Today, we are more than just business partners.
> We are friends. Edna and I routinely meet to
> discuss matters of mutual concern."

"Yes, they are magnificent creatures. I believe they are the largest land mammals on the planet."

"Indeed they are," Gregory said. "But with all their strength and size, there is one thing that they cannot do."

Charles thought carefully for a moment. "With all that mass, I guess the only thing they really can't do is jump."

"Close enough! Unlike the giraffes, they cannot reach the higher branches and leaves on a tree. Elephants need to use their magnificent tusks to knock down the trees. Once a tree is down, they eat the trunks of the trees, the bark, and the leaves and branches."

"So what did you do?" Charles asked.

"I walked slowly over to the herd's alpha female, the oldest and strongest elephant. I kept my head down slightly to show respect and indicate I was not being aggressive with my behavior. When I got close enough, I looked up to talk to her."

"You must have felt like I did when I looked up at you after drinking the water in the little pond. It hurt my neck to keep stretching it back to get you in view," Charles said.

Gregory smiled. "That is how I felt in her presence. Her tusks were enormous. If she wanted to, she could have slung me through the air like a ... uh ... a ..."

"Like a chimpanzee. It is okay to say it," Charles said.

Gregory appreciated that Charles was not the type to be slighted at some of his remarks. "Yes, like a chimp. Anyway, I introduced myself, and she said her name was Edna. We started talking, and I told her that maybe we could come up with a mutually beneficial arrangement. And that is what we have today. The elephants come by about once a week to help us knock down trees needed to continue our building or restoration efforts. In return, we give them all the limbs and bark products that we stripped during production. We also give them any trees that we could not use for construction because of size or a poor cut we made when splitting it."

Gil spoke up. "The younger apes think it is fun to race in teams, carrying the trees on their shoulders to the elephants. We even started an annual event when the whole community comes by to watch the race and cheer for their favorite teams. At the end, we crown the winning team as the annual champions. They get bragging rights, and it impresses the lady apes."

Gregory said, "Right, and Edna and the elephant community enjoy it as well. The young apes dress up in outlandish costumes, and we added obstacles they need to get over while carrying the logs. It really is a sight to see."

"More importantly." Gregory got serious. "Our jungle forests are not being ravaged as they once were. By cooperating, we get the trees we need for construction, and the elephants get what they need to eat. Today, we are more than just business partners. We are friends. Edna and I routinely meet to discuss matters of mutual concern. We recently built a shelter to keep the elderly, sick, and infant elephants out of the rain. Our apes also periodically patrol their communal area on the lookout for predators such as lions, tigers, hyenas, crocodiles, and even poisonous snakes like a king cobra."

"Yeah, a gorilla is too dumb to be afraid." Gil snorted.

"Hardly, our volunteer patrols are brave apes. Although we expect nothing in return, having a friendly herd of elephants in your neighboring community is a pretty good line of defense for us as well."

CHAPTER NINE

◆

In the Midst of Gorillas

> "A leader cannot take himself too seriously, Charles. I do not know your particular circumstances back in your environment. I do know that having fun in the workplace, doing a few backflips, is not a negative thing as long as it is controlled and the job is still being done."

After Gil's tree-cutting demo, Gregory and Charles left the branch chief's office and went around back to where the real work took place. Charles followed Gregory as he mixed it up with the younger apes.

"Gabe, I hear that you are wearing a purple dress in the next Tree Run through the Forest competition. Is that right?"

"No, Mr. Gregory. You must be mistaken me with Guy over there. I heard he wants to wear a purple dress this year to match his purple high-heel shoes."

"Yes, sir." Guy was quick to continue the good-natured ribbing. "I plan to wear a bright purple dress and purple high-heel shoes, and I might even wear a purple hat with a purple feather."

"Why all the purple, Guy?" Gregory asked. "Is that your favorite color?"

"No, sir. I figured I am going to be so far ahead of Gabe that I want to wear something bright so he can see me from a distance, you know, from way back."

Gregory saw an opportunity. "Listen up, all you young apes. If any team can break the six-minute barrier, I will show up at the awards ceremony in a pink dress."

Word quickly spread through the work yard that the alpha ape himself had thrown down a challenge. Some of the more assertive apes began thumping their chests with their mighty paws and began grunting loudly. Others began climbing up trees and doing backflips to the ground.

Charles thought to himself, *These apes may be big and strong, but they are not as graceful as Cliff when it comes to flying through the air.*

Gregory let the younger gorillas play out their bravado gestures for a few minutes before restoring order. "Okay, okay. You had better save your energy for the race. Just to be clear. I said you need to be under six minutes. The record time is six minutes and twenty-four seconds, so you got a long way to go before I go into my wife's closet to start trying on her dresses."

Gregory got serious. "Fun's over. Time to get back to work. Team, I want you to meet Charles from South Forest. He wants to see how you are able to turn these large trees into the foundation to build our Learning Center."

Gregory was pleased when they all gathered around Charles to say hello before dividing into their normal work units. As Charles walked through the different stages of production, the team leads were eager to explain their specific role in the process. Gregory was also impressed as he watched from a near distance that Charles showed keen interest and asked many questions, even though he had already heard the procedures from Gil during the demonstration in his office.

After Charles had patiently heard the last team's presentation, he thanked the entire group and joined Gregory as they walked away from the production site together.

As they were making their way back to the center of the compound, Charles stopped in his tracks. "Gregory, I am curious. Why did you do what you did back there with the young apes?"

Gregory, also stopping, asked Charles, "Can you elaborate a bit more?"

Charles had a puzzled look. "It just seems odd to me that you would take a peaceful setting and then deliberately turn it chaotic. Back in South Forest, I have the opposite objective. My chimps are already wired and swing through trees. My goal is to get them to be quiet and still."

Spotting a bench nearby, Gregory motioned for Charles to join him to continue their conversation more comfortably. "You are right, Charles. I did create a little chaos in the workplace. How long did it actually last? Five minutes maybe. At most about ten. Those apes are the backbone to our North Forest society. They build, they repair, they renovate, and they protect just by their presence. If you noticed, they were releasing some stress by their antics in response to my challenge. Work can be tedious, even dangerous at times. Dawson's accident is a prime example. Although the young apes appear strong and dominant on the outside, they still have their vulnerabilities and times of self-doubt. It is ape nature.

"So if I tease with them a bit, make them laugh, and issue a challenge that they will honestly probably never meet, it rejuvenates them. It gives them something to look forward to as individuals and team members. The young apes will probably spend a little more time at the gym or running around the track to do their best. I hope they will get together as a team more often and practice their stride and tree-carrying technique. The worst that can happen is that I wear a pink dress for an hour or two. Big deal.

"A leader cannot take himself too seriously, Charles. I do not know your particular circumstances back in your environment. I do know that having fun in the workplace, doing a few backflips, is not a negative thing, as long as it is controlled and the job is still being done. Do you understand what I am telling you?"

Charles was deep in thought, thinking about his staff meetings and rethinking what Gregory was telling him. "Yes, I do see what you mean. Thanks for sharing."

"Actually, I cannot take credit for that tip. Edna, the elephant herd leader, shared that with me one day. She had done something similar, not exactly of course, with her young elephants. Learning from a wise leader like Edna is a real gift for me."

"I am sure Edna learns as much from you as you do with her," Charles declared.

"Perhaps, but Edna has survived in this jungle twice the years that I have been in it. One of my favorite moments is to just spend time with Edna and talk about leadership. You need somebody to confide in and bounce ideas off of, my friend."

Charles replied thoughtfully, "Yes, of course. That makes sense."

Before Gregory could continue, two young apes descended on him. "Uncle Gregory! Give me a ride on your big shoulders!"

"Grover, wait a second. You are being rude by not acknowledging my guest here, Charles."

"I am sorry, Gregory. Yes, I apologize."

"Grover, Galileo, I want you to meet Charles."

"Charles, these two strapping apes are Grover and Galileo."

"Nice to meet you, Mr. Charles," both of them said in unison.

Soon, the brothers were taking turns riding on Gregory's back, frolicking and wrestling on the ground with him. Charles could only smile as he watched the alpha ape who seemed to enjoy himself as much as the younger pair did.

"All right, you two win. Now go home before your mom, Bethany, lets me have it. She will beat me up if you are late for lunch. Get moving."

The brother apes laughed in harmony at the thought of their mom being able to beat up the strongest ape in North Forest. "Okay, Uncle Gregory. It was nice meeting you, Mr. Charles," Galileo and Grover said in accord as they hurried off.

"I have the feeling that you are Uncle Gregory to scores of young apes in North Forest, not just Grover and Galileo," Charles said, teasing Gregory.

"Yes, I see our future when I look into their eyes. That is why arranging the deal we made with the elephants was so important. At the rate the elephants were knocking down trees, there would be no wood for any building to keep up with our population growth."

Gregory started walking toward the western part of the complex. As Charles followed closely behind, he wondered if Gregory forgot that they were going to the educational facility to see the impressive five-story structure. He caught himself and realized he was not being courteous of Gregory's time. After all, they had spent quite a bit of time with Gil and the younger apes to see the production process.

At first, Charles thought they were going to visit the mayor's office, but Gregory kept walking past the building. Directly behind it was an even larger building with a sign in front that read "Modern Jungle Construction Company—Administrative Offices."

When they entered the building, Charles could feel the electricity in the air that followed Gregory's arrival. As the founder and owner of MJC2, as Andreas had referred to it, Gregory clearly was a respected and beloved leader.

As he moved his large frame to peek into the various offices, such as ape resources and procurement, his employees greeted him with a smile and sometimes a quick embrace. In all cases, Gregory motioned to Charles and properly introduced his guest.

DEVELOPING YOUR
GORILLA QUOTIENT (GQ):
SECOND REFLECTION

Leaders should not feel threatened by others

Gregory could have taken a completely different approach upon first meeting Charles at the small pool where the chimpanzee had gone to refresh himself. Gregory may well have viewed Charles as a trespasser on North Forest gorilla territory. Imagine the poor chimpanzee's reaction to see a charging seven hundred-pound gorilla coming straight at him.

Instead, Gregory did not feel or act threatened. Why should he? After all, he was the alpha ape. As a result, the gorilla was gracious and welcoming to his visitor, and in the end, Gregory benefited from Charles' perspective and insight. That is what great (or big) leaders do, feel confident enough in their own abilities and always open to learn from others.

Gregory reached out to Edna and the elephant herd to solve mutual concerns in a way that was nonthreatening. Too often, we see those in other organizations as a threat and view them from a zero-sum game perspective. If they succeed or look good, we somehow fail or look bad.

In reality, results, regardless who gets the credit for an idea, measures a leader's performance. Whenever possible, seek partnerships in endeavors. A rising tide lifts all boats.

Demonstrate accountability

The only time a leader should say "I" is to pronounce "I messed up" or "I assume full responsibility." Otherwise, it should be "we," which demonstrates a team approach. Do not be concerned with covering up your mistakes. Your followers understand that you are human and a leadership role is not easy. When you continue to deny or deflect responsibility when mistakes happen, you only lose credibility along the way. Instead of appearing big, a leader diminishes in stature.

When Gregory's assistant, Andreas, tried to cover for his boss for Dawson's accident, the alpha ape clearly did not follow his well-intentioned lead. Recall Gregory's words. "Andreas, I am the one with the final signature. As far as I am concerned, I am accountable for Dawson's accident, not some piece of equipment." The large ape remained large.

Recently, I served as the chief financial officer for the Food Safety Inspection Service Agency in Washington DC, part of the Department of Agriculture. Those two years were especially challenging with the fiscal uncertainty and austerity that came with the budget cuts known as sequestration.

On one occasion, I provided less than accurate budget data to the agency's administrator during one of our private meetings. Frankly, I had gotten ahead of my staff that had provided me preliminary numbers but had warned me they were still running through the necessary calculations before having a final figure.

This was an unforced error on my part. In addition to providing poor advice to the administrator, I also made the budget staff look bad. When the updated budget-related calculation was ready, it was significantly off from my earlier estimate. At that point, I could let it go and provide the new data to my boss over time to minimize my mistake. However, that would be unfair to both him and my staff.

I quickly arranged for a second meeting the same day with the administrator, but I invited the two senior budget directors to the meeting this time. In my boss' office, I told him that it was my fault, not my staff, for prematurely providing important budgetary information. I apologized to him and my team and promised to do better in the future. Fortunately, my boss was gracious in his response, as was the crew. Demonstrating accountability is often difficult but necessary as a leader.

Joseph L. Garcia

A leader should occasionally lighten the mood

Actor John Cleese (voice of King Harold in the *Shrek* movies) once observed, "I think the main evolutionary significance of our sense of humor is that it gets us from the closed mode to the open mode quicker than anything else. I think we all know laugher brings relaxation and humor makes us playful."[4]

An effective leader recognizes the need to lighten the mood to keep employees engaged and to release the stress that builds up over time. Recognizing this, Gregory seized an opportunity in the logistics work yard when he good-humoredly teased some of the apes about the next Tree Run through the Forest competition. The young apes responded enthusiastically to their leader, and as a result, positive energy was created in the work yard.

Puzzled by his actions, Charles later asked Gregory why he turned a peaceful setting situation into a chaotic one. Gregory's response is telling. "So if I tease with them a bit, make them laugh, and issue a challenge that they will honestly probably never meet, it rejuvenates them. It gives them something to look forward to, as individuals and team members." As to the consequence for the leader, the alpha ape replied, "The worst that can happen is that I wear a pink dress for an hour or two. Big deal."

Years ago, I taught a leadership class to upper-division cadets at the Air Force Academy in Colorado Springs, Colorado. On one occasion, I coordinated an idea with a lieutenant assigned to work with me. (He was a recent Academy graduate awaiting orders to attend flight school.)

The morning of the leadership session, I handed the lieutenant a videotape to show at the beginning of the class. The tape contained a five-minute cartoon that I had recorded over the weekend. It was one of those clips that you could not help but laugh at, slapstick humor with the characters' eyes popping out or jaws dropping to the ground. It was silly but funny.

---

[4] John Cleese, "And Now for Something Completely Different," *Management Review*, May 1991, 50–53.

I arranged for the lieutenant to walk into the classroom, take attendance, and then tell them that I was issuing them a challenge. The challenge was to determine the significance of the cartoon they were about to see. If they got it right, I would eliminate one of the ten mandatory journal entries that was a class requirement.

The "LT" got the cartoon clip going and stepped back to watch the group interact. As expected, the students were soon laughing at the animation while at the same time trying to analyze the cartoon itself. They were searching for a deeper meaning of the cartoon story line or characters. They had boxed themselves in with their line of thinking.

When I arrived, I asked the group for their consensus on what the significance of the cartoon was. After hearing their ideas, I gave them the answer that I was really seeking. The cartoon itself was actually insignificant. It was the purpose behind showing it. I shared with the cadets that they would soon be entering active duty as second lieutenants as leaders of men and women.

Their cadet training tended to emphasize order and discipline. The population they managed (other cadets) was within the physical constraints of the Academy itself. Soon, they would be leading a more diverse group of people. The purpose of showing them the five-minute video was to break up the class monotony, do something a bit different, and stimulate their thinking ability.

The formal lesson that day was actually a good one on the importance of values. My intention was to generate another important lesson for the cadets, that is, it was okay for a leader to have a sense of humor and a little fun as a means to connect with followers and get creative juices flowing. In the manner, that Gregory had done with the young apes in the work yard.

CHAPTER TEN

◆

Gregory's Deputy

> "Gregory has taught me that being a good leader
> does not always mean needing to be out in front."

As they were near the end of the large hallway, a voice proclaimed, "Welcome, boss. I heard you were on your way. This must be Charles behind you. Greetings, Charles, and welcome to our facility and North Forest community. My name is Kayla. I am Gregory's deputy."

"Charles, Kayla actually runs the place. She tells me where to be, who to meet, and what to sign. I just go along for the ride." Gregory laughed.

Turning serious, Kayla pulled Gregory aside and lowered her voice. "Per your request, Ryan and the rest of the union representatives are gathered in the conference room. I told them that you were still reviewing all options involving Dawson after the accident. This meeting was to discuss more than that incident."

Gregory nodded his head in agreement. "Right, we need to talk in general about career progression for the younger apes. I want to make sure that Ryan understands my feelings about how important education is for the workforce. Although plenty of brawn is involved in doing most of the heavy construction work, the apes need to develop their brains too. The jobs will always be there. I do not want them dropping out of college to get on the payroll. If necessary, we can develop part-time employment so they can pursue both work and their degrees."

"Are you sure you don't need me in the meeting with you?" Kayla asked.

"No thanks, Kayla. I prefer to do this one myself. You can do me a big favor though. I promised Charles that we would actually see the education complex. He is very interested in the layout. Unfortunately, we got behind schedule a bit visiting the production facility with Gil. While I am in this meeting, it should take an hour, have Professor Gaylord show him around the Learning Center and then take him back to my office. Please ask Andreas to prepare lunch for Charles and me. We can eat when I return."

"Of course," Kayla told her boss. "Don't worry. I will take good care of Charles here. Concentrate on your meeting with the union. I do need to talk to you about the new Self-Review Program, but we can do that later this afternoon." Gregory walked to his right, knocked on the door, and then entered the conference room.

Kayla led the visitor to her office and offered Charles a seat on the couch. "Charles, I took the liberty of arranging for some refreshments. Sorry. It is not ants and bananas, but the fresh berries are very good. You can wash them down with this mango juice. After a short break, I will escort you to the education facility."

Charles paused a moment and then asked in bewilderment, "How did you know what I liked to eat or, for that matter, even that we were coming to the building?"

Kayla smiled in return. "Actually, news can travel quickly through the complex. You were with Gregory when he challenged the young apes to beat the record and he would wear a pink dress. The two events—your presence and Gregory's challenge—became one in the message."

Charles was grateful for the refreshments. It had been awhile since he had eaten a few grasshoppers for breakfast. "Kayla, may I ask you a question?"

"Fire away," Kayla replied.

"What exactly does a deputy do? I am not even familiar with that term."

Kayla smiled. "That is another bit of news that has preceded you. The word in the compound is that Gregory feels you ask very thought-provoking questions. He actually admires that about you. Gregory often says that a right answer is important, but the right question is better.

"As deputy, I serve at the will of Gregory, but he has essentially delegated certain areas of the business to me. If you noticed the sign in front of the building, here are the administrative functions such as ape resources, procurement, accounting, and safety. That is why I have my office here. Gregory tends to concentrate on operations—the actual building and maintenance of North Forest structures—because that is the core of our business. He, along with Gil, built it from scratch. I also assist Gregory with planning and budgeting. He is confident in himself to know his own limits in both capacity and natural gifts. We work well together as a team. Whenever there is a meeting and he is not present, I have his full confidence to speak for him."

Charles carefully took in what she told him. Kayla could see another question coming her way shortly. She waited patiently in the meantime.

"What is the most important trait that a deputy should have to be successful?" Charles finally asked.

Her quick response time surprised him. "The ability to listen."

"That is not the answer I expected. You just described a deputy as someone who takes plenty of action so her boss can have less on his plate. If you are listening, you are not really doing anything. I would think that a deputy, being second in command, is a doer, not a passive bystander."

Kayla went over to a board on one side of her office and began writing:

- Learn from others
- Instill pride of ownership
- Share the center stage
- Teamwork is promoted
- Ego is kept in check
- New ideas are created

She then underlined the first letter of each sentence, which spelled the word "listen."

"Gregory has taught me that being a good leader does not always mean needing to be out in front. I admit that, when he hired me for the deputy position, I had a different attitude. I mistakenly felt that I had to make every decision. However, in so doing, I was stifling growth and creativity among the other apes. Gregory leads by example in this area."

Again, Charles grew quiet. *Maybe this is what Cyrus was trying to tell me when he told me he hoped I'd better not be eaten by a lion or the place would fall apart. Am I a good listener? Maybe it was not the other chimps like Cliff, Ava, and Autumn that were at fault. It might be that I am too quick to take action ahead of them.*

"You know what I really find amazing, Kayla. It's how a towering ape like Gregory is so disciplined to not act like the alpha ape, even though everyone knows he is one. He seems to hold back from being dominant—not in a passive way—but ... restrained."

Charles noticed a change in Kayla's expression as she got up and faced out the window. *Have I spoken inappropriately? Hopefully not. Again, I am very grateful for the hospitality the whole community has shown to me.*

"Charles, I believe I can trust you with something that very few apes know about Gregory. He seems to trust you."

"I greatly appreciate how Gregory has treated me today. I would never do anything that harms our relationship. My hope is that we can continue to be friends after I return to South Forest."

Kayla walked back to sit next to Charles. "Gregory moved to North Forest many years ago. He lived in a forest far away from here. His father was even larger than Gregory is today, and unfortunately, he did act every bit the alpha ape. The trouble is that there are sometimes multiple alpha apes, at least in their minds. We do not have that problem here, primarily because Gregory is not one to be looking to challenge others who might challenge him.

"The dominant alpha ape was getting older, so some of the younger ones were beginning to position themselves to take over at the right moment. Gregory's father was one of those contenders, and he had a few enemies in the village. Charles, have you ever seen two adult gorillas fight? I do not mean a brief skirmish, but a real battle."

"No, I have only seen gorillas from afar until today," Charles noted.

"It started when Gregory's father bumped into another one of the leading apes by not giving ground. They both started pounding their chest and screaming loud roars, and most often, both apes back down with pride intact. In this case, a large crowd had gathered, and there was no escape. My mother happened to be at the scene, so I am telling you what happened from someone who was actually there."

Kayla slowly shook her head. "Charles, when two large gorillas fight for real, someone is going to get hurt. In the end, Gregory's father died during the violent encounter. The other ape, although victorious, did not fare any better. He also perished a few days later because of the wounds inflicted by Gregory's father.

"Fortunately, Gregory was not at the immediate scene when it happened, but of course, he found out about it. And when he finally joined the commotion, his father lay still in front of him. Gregory could have become bitter and followed his father's footsteps, consumed with anger and violence. Instead, Gregory only saw it as a great waste. He did not make a fallen warrior out of his father. When he was older, he left his home village and came to North Forest to get away from the difficult memories.

"Perhaps you can see now why Gregory tries to keep his emotions and ego in check. He knows it runs through his blood from his father, but he will not follow his father's destructive behavior. Trust me. Gregory is a fierce warrior and fighter. Awhile back, two marauding lions entered North Forest early in the morning before most of the gorillas were up and about. Fortunately, Gregory encountered them and chased them off. He is a fearless ape. The other gorillas know that and give him lots of room. However, he wants peace whenever possible. He hates the waste that comes with conflict."

Charles could only shake his head at what Kayla had told him. "Thank you for sharing that information. I will not violate your trust."

"I know you won't," Kayla replied. "We'd better get moving to the education facility and then get you to his office on time. Gregory may be a congenial ape, but you had still better follow his direction. He is not a pushover by any means."

As they left through the back door of the building, they walked eastward along the trail that connected all sides in a rectangle shape. The path apparently served as a walkway to the various buildings and an exercise route as well. Many apes were along the trail. Most they encountered on the path were quick to offer Kayla and Charles a hearty greeting. It was strange to Charles, but he felt at home in this community. Gregory deserved the credit for going out of his way to spend time and energy on his visitor.

They were near the education facility when Charles noticed to his left several apes gathered around a large vat of some kind.

Slowing down to take in the scene, Kayla motioned to him. "Come on. I think you might find this interesting."

"What is going on, my young primates?" Kayla bellowed.

The apes stood erect from their hunched positions and turned to face Kayla and Charles.

After quick introductions, Kayla pointed to the leader of the group. "Nathan, please take a moment and tell our visitor what he is looking at and the role your crew plays at North Forest."

"Certainly, Kayla. Hello, Charles. Welcome. What you see in front of you is a large container of water. It is too high for you to see over, but if you climb up that ladder, you can look over to see for yourself."

Nathan waited until Charles had reached the top and was looking down into the large cylinder before continuing.

"Gregory realized awhile back that, with all of the wood buildings being built in the compound, we had a risk of fire caused by lightning hitting the nearby trees or the structure itself. He asked the mayor to hold a town hall meeting down in the amphitheater over there to raise the concern. He did not want to raise a panic but merely present the problem. To make a long story short, the mayor called for volunteers to establish a committee to look for options to address the risk."

"Nathan is being modest, Charles. He actually headed the committee and came up with the solution," Kayla said with pride in her voice.

"Well, it was definitely a team effort," Nathan replied. "What we eventually came up with was building a number of these cisterns placed strategically throughout the compound. This one here is located to deal with a potential fire in the Learning Center. We located them slightly to the back of each structure so it would not be an eyesore."

"If there is a fire, how in the world would you ever get the water from here to there?" Charles pointed to the water. "I know your Mighty Jungle coconut juice cups are big, but it would take a lot of apes running from this container using those cups to put out a fire." He soon had the apes rolling on the ground as he bounced his hands up and down, pretending to hold a cup to make his point.

Nathan stepped up, still laughing himself. "No, sir. The gorillas would not put out a fire. Our elephant friends would help us. You see, we have a designated ape whose job is to be ready to run full speed to notify the herd if we need assistance. The elephants would rush back here, reach in with their massive trunks to the appropriate container, and douse out the fire. We of course tested it by building a structure and then putting it on fire. You would be surprised how far they can spray the water."

Charles thought, *CHIMP Inc. might be able to improve on that arrangement.*

But he did not bring it up. Instead, he said, "Very impressive. That is a very innovative solution."

"Thank you, sir," Nathan replied. "Coming from the chimp executive officer of an innovation company, I will take that as a big compliment."

On second thought … Charles mused inwardly. *They seem to be communicating just fine without Virtual Vine. Still, the chimps might be able to save them valuable time for something as serious as putting out a fire. It could even mean saving a gorilla life.*

After saying their farewells, Kayla led Charles back toward the trail that took them to the front of the education building. At last, he would be able to go inside the massive structure that had made such an impression on him from the moment Gregory pointed it out.

CHAPTER ELEVEN

◆

The Learning Center

> "At the Learning Center, we also teach character development. The ability to trust each other, to be honest, and to place others before self is the cornerstone our society builds upon above all others."

"Ah, Professor Gaylord, thank you for meeting with us. I present to you—"

Before Kayla could even finish her sentence, the professor bowed and said, "Mr. Charles, it is indeed a pleasure. Welcome to our Learning Center."

Kayla persisted. "Professor Gaylord is a distinguished professor at our college, but he is also responsible for the entire education system from our elementary and middle schools to the high school and college programs. We found that one person, instead of four separate headmasters, seems to integrate the learning better along the continuum."

"Come, Charles." The professor put his hand on the chimp's shoulder. "You can observe some of our classroom training. I alerted a few teachers, and they are eager to show you their stuff. You know, a teacher is no different from the thespians that perform at the theater. There is a certain thrill to being in front of an audience. At the auditorium, the audience are the patrons of the arts. In the classroom, the audiences are the students."

Kayla and Charles followed the professor into the back of one of the classrooms. The instructor briefly looked their way and gave a slight nod of acknowledgement. Two students appeared to be in a debate of some kind. Professor Gaylord pressed close to Charles and began to whisper, "In this exercise, Sean, the student on the left, is being punished for cheating. The one on the right, Gilda, turned in her friend to the teacher. Sean is asking her why she did so if they were friends."

Charles nodded his head, but he could not figure out what kind of learning was going on here. At South Forest, they kept to the fundamentals of math and sciences.

After a few minutes, the teacher excused the two students and waited until they sat down. She looked at the class and asked simply, "Did Gilda do the right thing, or was she wrong to turn in her friend Sean?"

A flurry of ape hands shot in the air, hoping the teacher called on them to respond to the question.

"Gilda should have kept quiet. She had no business telling on Sean," one student said.

"Sean is the one who cheated. Sooner or later, he was going to get caught," another student spoke, countering.

As other students engaged in the spirited debate, the professor motioned for Kayla and Charles to exit the way they had come in. Charles shook his head as he told the professor, "I have to admit. Classes in South Forest are nothing like that one in there."

The professor grinned slightly, clearly pleased that Charles had made that particular statement. "We teach the courses that most other schools do. The young apes need to know about history, geography, and language. At the Learning Center, we also teach character development. The ability to trust each other, to be honest, and to place others before self is the cornerstone our society builds upon above all others."

Professor Gaylord stepped into an empty classroom, went to a board, and quickly drew a graph.

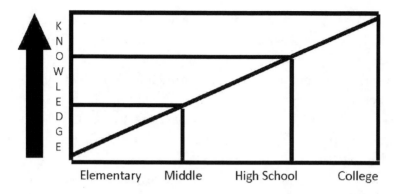

"Charles, make no mistake. Our goal is that, as the young apes progress through the education system, their general knowledge increases accordingly. Our test results clearly support that goal is being met. A primate attending college is sure to know more than one in middle school or high school. Their brains are more developed, and the years at the Learning Center stretch their learning capacity.

"However, from the very first day of school, we want our apes to learn the difference between right and wrong. Therefore, character should not be on an upward sloping line, as is general knowledge. It should instead be on a straight line—constant."

He proceeded to draw a second graph to show it to Charles visually.

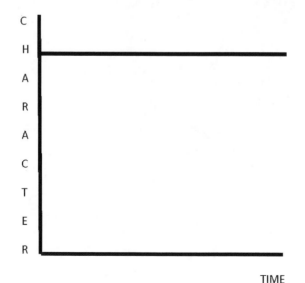

"Yes, of course, I can see the difference now," Charles said.

As Kayla and Charles followed the professor into the different grades of the Learning Center, he did notice how the precision-cut trees formed a smooth floor surface at each floor level. Originally, he was most interested in the physical magnitude of the building from the outside. As they ended the tour of the Learning Center, Charles gained an appreciation for what was happening inside the construction project, not the structure itself.

After thanking Professor Gaylord, Charles followed Kayla across the center of the compound as they headed back toward Gregory's office.

"Well, Charles, you certainly have seen a full spectrum of activities in a short time so far at North Forest. You saw the ape power of Gil's production line and the brainpower of Professor Gaylord's Learning Center. What impressed you more?"

After a moment, Charles replied, "That both can go on at the same time and at the same place. I guess the balance itself is the most impressive to me."

"Well said," Kayla said softly.

◆

Chapter Twelve

The Gorilla Way

Gregory brought his mighty shoulders back and fully squared himself. As he headed toward the door, he muttered, "I will return shortly. Tell Hannah to wait for me."

As Kayla and Charles entered the main office of the North Forest Construction Company, Andreas was busy placing refreshments in the reception area for them.

"Greetings!" the broad-shouldered young ape exclaimed at seeing them both.

Charles thought, *This is one energetic gorilla. His upbeat attitude never wavers.*

"The boss is still with the union, but he sent word that he should be heading back soon." Andreas conveyed to Kayla. Then he turned his attention to Charles. "Did you enjoy the tour of the Learning Center? Professor Gaylord is a brilliant ape. He was one of my favorite college instructors. I also see that you visited the fire prevention facility. Pretty impressive, huh?"

Charles walked over to where Andreas had placed the afternoon pick-me-up. As he helped himself to a serving, he looked up at the young primate who was standing in front of him.

"Tell me, Andreas. What type of communication system exists that keeps you so updated on our whereabouts?" Charles smiled. "We just left the Learning Center and headed straight over to this building. I did not notice any gorillas going to or coming from the office. Come on. Tell me your secret."

Andreas stepped to the side. "When I said I see you visited the Learning Center and the fire prevention facility, that is what I meant."

Charles looked out the window that had a straight view to both venues. "Oh," was all that he could muster.

Don't I feel like a chimp, he thought.

Just then, Gregory walked in the door. "Sorry that I am late and made you wait. Andreas, is Hannah stopping by soon?"

"Yes, sir. She should be here shortly."

"Good. Kayla, Charles, please come in. We can catch up." Gregory motioned the odd-looking pair into his office.

Kayla, the smaller female of the gorilla species, still towered over their visitor from South Forest.

Before Gregory could sit down, Kayla eagerly queried him, "How did the union meeting go, Gregory? Good or bad?"

"Actually, our time together went quite well. It even went over our allotted time," Gregory said proudly as he sat behind his large desk. "It took a while, but I think we had a major breakthrough."

"What was the breakthrough?" Charles asked.

"Talking and listening," Gregory succinctly replied.

Kayla winked at Charles as they both thought of their earlier conversation in her office about Gregory's emphasis on the ability to listen.

Gregory apparently did not notice the nonverbal exchange, as he continued unabated. "Ryan is an ape like anyone else. He comes on a bit strong at times, but I learned something new about him today. Ryan agrees with the need to keep the younger primates in college longer than they are staying now. He was merely going along with them joining the union because he felt they were more vulnerable to lower-paying jobs without the advantage that the guild provides."

"In other words ..." Gregory leaned forward. "He wants to protect the apes, not use them for his benefit. Ryan, along with the others, is looking for some guarantee that the jobs will be waiting for the younger apes if they stay in college long enough to graduate."

"How can you be sure that is his real intention?" Kayla asked.

"Oh, I am convinced. I have never really questioned Ryan's integrity, perhaps just his tactics," Gregory responded. "No, what swayed me was when Ryan brought up his own apes. He is a concerned father and wants only the best for them. Ryan never even finished high school. He wants his brood to do better than he did. He wants a management program established at the college so graduates can move faster through the career leader. His oldest one is about to finish high school." Gregory laughed. "Ryan said he knows that Gil and I won't be around forever and we need new blood in the corporation to keep it going."

"He didn't!" Kayla gasped.

"Yes, he did. And you know what? He is exactly right."

Charles sat quietly, trying not to intrude in the conversation between Gregory and Kayla. He did take mental notes regarding how the education programs at South Forest could better integrate with the workforce needs.

Gregory leaned back in his chair and relaxed for a moment before readdressing Kayla. "You mentioned you needed to talk to me about the Self-Review Program. All the units were given a deadline to complete them by the end of the week. Tomorrow is Friday, so what is the status?"

Kayla looked at Charles before answering Gregory. "Charles, after Dawson's accident, Gregory felt that there should be a means to learn from any mistakes or missteps. Therefore, he initiated a Self-Inspection or Self-Review Program. Each functional area, like logistics, procurement, AR, and so forth, did a risk analysis and was told to develop a set of questions that they would self-report on semiannually."

Charles interjected, "That sounds like a great idea, but how do you know their self-reporting will be honest and objective? It seems like ape nature to not convey any problems to upper management."

"Another brilliant question, Charles." The alpha ape pointed his mammoth index finger toward the chimpanzee guest. "That is where Kayla and her staff will come in. They will randomly review responses to ensure they are credible and valid."

Kayla paused a moment.

"Okay, Deputy, tell me what is wrong. I know your body language by now, and something is amiss."

69

"Well, boss," Kayla sighed, "the good news is that all but one of the units has completed their initial set of self-review questions ahead of schedule. I took a quick look, and for the most part, they are good. They deserve credit for complying with your intent of the program."

Gregory got up from his chair and walked around his desk to get closer to Kayla.

"Let me guess. Hannah asked for a few extra days to get them exactly right. She is nearly a perfectionist when it comes to her work."

Kayla shook her head slightly. "No, sir. It wasn't Hannah. Hers were on time, and she had one of the best submissions. Like you stated, she is meticulous with her work."

"Hmmm. That would have been my only guess that makes sense. All the staff knows how strong I feel about establishing an internal review, especially after the accident." Gregory paced in front of the window with his hand on his chin. "I give up, Kayla. Tell me."

Charles felt uncomfortable being in the same room during this conversation. It reminded him about when he was a young chimp at the dinner table and his parents were having an argument. He could not leave without asking permission, but he knew better than to interrupt, so he was stuck with no place to go.

After another pause, Kayla finally looked at Gregory and said quietly, "Gil."

Gregory stopped pacing and looked at Kayla. "Excuse me. I did not hear you."

"It is Gil, sir. He may not meet the deadline."

"How close is he to finishing?" Gregory asked.

Kayla stood up out of respect to Gregory to continue the difficult conversation at eye level. "I asked him the same thing this morning because it is due tomorrow. Every time I inquired about it, he would always say that he was working on it. As you know, Gil does tend to get administrative tasks completed at the last second. Today, however, Gil complained that he thought it was a waste of time. He felt the accident was a fluke thing and the whole program was an overreaction to a single event. He had other projects that needed his focus. Gil said you would understand and that he was not worried about it."

Gregory brought his mighty shoulders back and fully squared himself. As he headed toward the door, he muttered, "I will return shortly. Tell Hannah to wait for me."

Charles watched as Gregory carefully closed the door behind him. It was as if the lion chaser's natural instinct were to slam the door with enough force to collapse the whole room. Instead, he deliberately took the time and effort to shut the door with only a light clicking sound.

Kayla and Charles sat silently for a few awkward moments before the chimp spoke.

"What do you think will happen?" he asked.

Kayla shook her head slightly. "I do not know, Charles. Of all gorillas not to support the program, Gil is the last ape that Gregory would expect. I am afraid to say it, but I think Gil took advantage of their friendship."

CHAPTER THIRTEEN

Ape Resources (AR)

> "My team and I ensure that the right ape is on the right
> job at the right time. Yes, that pretty much covers it."

Charles heard laughter coming from the front office. He walked over to the door and opened it slightly to see Andreas talking to an ape that he had not met yet. He could only assume that it was Hannah because she was scheduled to meet with Gregory.

Kayla, having regained her composure from the conversation regarding Gil, fully opened the door and gently put her large hand on the chimp's shoulder. "Come on, Charles. I want you to meet Hannah."

Andreas and Hannah were still engaged in light banter when she noticed the other two approaching them. "Hi, Kayla, and this must be Charles. It is certainly a pleasure to meet you."

Kayla stepped up to formally introduce them. "Charles, I would like you to meet Hannah. She is the head of ape resources, or AR, as we call it. Hannah, this is our special guest from South Forest, Charles."

"I feel like I already know you, Hannah. I have heard so much about you throughout the day, and all of it good of course," Charles said.

She quickly returned the compliment. "And I you, Charles. The whole compound seems to have caught Charles fever."

"It surely must be the novelty of being the only chimp in North Forest. There is nothing special about me," Charles stated modestly.

"Hardly." Hannah turned her attention to Kayla. "I saw Gregory heading back toward the logistics area. I was going to call out to him, but he seemed to be in a serious state of mind. Is everything okay?"

"Yes, he just needed to run down and speak to Gil about a pressing issue. He said he would be right back." Kayla did not feel it proper to go into any of the details.

"Well then, that would give me a little time to speak to our celebrity here." She pointed to Charles as they all converged back to Gregory's office.

Andreas peeked in only to announce, "Gregory asked me to run a special errand for him. I will be back shortly."

As Charles took a seat, he looked up at the two female gorillas and thought of his own wife for a moment. *I wonder how Taylor is doing and if she is worried about me.* For that matter, he felt guilty for spending the day so far away when he still had a company to run.

"Charles, do you agree?" Kayla appeared to be asking for a second time.

Charles shook his head abruptly. "I am sorry, Kayla. What are you asking me?"

"I was telling Hannah how amazing it is that you and Gregory hit it off so well. You act like old friends around each other, very naturally," Kayla replied patiently.

"Yes, of course. Gregory and the whole community in fact have been very cordial during my visit. Time has gone by pretty quickly today." Back in the moment, he focused his attention on the new gorilla. "Tell me, Hannah, what exactly does the head of ape resources do?"

"Let's see." Hannah rolled her eyes upward and tapped her right index finger to her left one. "My team and I ensure that the right ape is on the right job at the right time. Yes, that pretty much covers it."

Kayla jumped in the conversation. "Charles, the AR manager is a very important member of Gregory's MJC2 inner circle. Hannah is just being modest. She deals with all aspects of ape resources, from recruiting, hiring, training, retention, employee-management issues, benefits, and even retirement."

Charles took in Kayla's comments and reflected on what he had heard. He thought a moment more and then asked, "Hannah, from your unique perspective, what does management do right, and what does management do wrong when it comes to fully leveraging ape resources?"

"Well, first of all, I see it is true what Gregory and others say about you. Your questions are insightful and profound," Hannah responded. "By now, you know that Gregory is the founder and owner of our company. He is the alpha ape who sets the tone with his own leadership style. Gregory takes care of the mission and his employees and does not take his own position too seriously. He has a sense of humility and genuineness that others respond to. They see him as real."

Kayla also weighed in. "Charles, I am fond of Gregory as both a boss and a friend. You can respect the position but not always the ape. In Gregory's case, it is easy to follow him in both roles."

Charles nodded in agreement but continued to press Hannah. "Yes, I think we are in complete agreement about Gregory's leadership talent. However, he cannot be everywhere at once. As the AR manager, what works at the middle management echelon?"

Hannah did not hesitate. "Communication is the key at all levels, but like you say, especially in middle management and the frontline supervision. The managerial apes who are effective communicators are effective leaders. The effective leaders get results."

"Okay." Charles got up to retrieve more refreshments that Andreas had left for them. "What makes a good boss a good communicator? Is it holding organized staff meetings?"

Hannah said, "Not necessarily. I know some branch chiefs who rarely hold a staff meeting, but they keep their employees informed and engaged. A good leader works hard at communication. It is not easy to make that extra effort. Most of the problems I see that cross my desk can be traced back to those managers that either are poor communicators or do not attempt to communicate in the first place. Rather than making a good effort on their end, poor managers just blame the followers for not getting the message.

"Yet, a leader is primarily responsible for two-thirds of the basic communication system, the initial sender of the message and the message itself. The poor follower is the receiver, the third component of the communication system. In my book, if you hold two-thirds of the equation compared to one-third, then you need to do the majority lifting of the communication effort."

Kayla raised her hand. "Hannah, may I add something?"

"Of course, Kayla. Please do."

Kayla said, "Hannah is spot-on with her analysis. Good leaders do need to work hard to communicate, to train, to motivate, and to do all of those things. However, to be fair to them, I do expect the employees, the followers, to also be proactive in the process, especially when it comes to communication."

"How so?" asked Charles.

"Look at it this way." Kayla proceeded to the board in Gregory's office.

My goodness, Charles thought, *apes really like to draw out things on boards. I never would have guessed that before meeting them.*

Kayla drew a straight line across the board and then two ape figures on both ends.

Manager   Employee

Underneath the ape on the left, she wrote the word "manager." For the ape on the right, she wrote "employee." She said, "Because they are on the same plane, under normal circumstances, if they were to meet in the middle ..." She drew a star to designate that spot. "It would be an equal effort, wouldn't it?"

"That seems right to me," Charles said.

"But is it really fair?" Kayla questioned Charles. "I know our employees have plenty to do, and I have the highest regard for our ape force. They are truly the backbone of our community. Yet, the employee ape is primarily only responsible for himself or herself."

Kayla pointed at the manager ape. "The manager is responsible for many other ape employees, a budget, a higher boss, deadlines to meet, supplier negotiations, customer complaint resolutions, report writing, and much more." Kayla erased the manager ape and redrew the figure. "Therefore, I contend that the manager ape, by virtue of more responsibilities, should be put up a notch compared to the employee ape, just as he or she would be on an org chart."

Manager

Employee

Kayla then changed the line connecting manager and employee apes to reflect a downward slope. "Now if they were to still meet in the middle, as this new graph shows, the employee ape must work harder than the manager ape because he or she is going slightly uphill." As Kayla sat down to rejoin them, she looked smugly at Charles. "Well, what do you think?"

Charles thought a moment. "I think you should ask Professor Gaylord to get you some art lessons."

DEVELOPING YOUR
GORILLA QUOTIENT (GQ):
THIRD REFLECTION

The right answer is important, but the right question is better

An effective leader seeks continuous improvement and strategic solutions, not patchwork fixes. Kayla shared with the visiting chimpanzee that Gregory often said that, while a right answer is important, the right question was even better. The alpha ape has a point worth further reflection.

Gregory's Mighty Jungle Construction Company (or MJC2) had built infrastructure throughout North Forest over time, using the trees felled by their elephant partners. The alpha ape realized that, although there was much to celebrate in the new wooden structures, there was an inherent risk to fire caused by lightning.

Instead of looking for a quick fix to the potential fire issue, Gregory encouraged the mayor to engage the community to develop a long-term strategy. Notice that, after Gregory provided the initial problem statement, he quickly retreated so others could step in. As a result, Nathan led a committee of volunteers that eventually produced the system of cisterns throughout the complex. They even engaged their elephant neighbors to assist in the outcome.

If a problem arises, dig deeper for potential root causes to the dilemma. When possible, be patient. Keep the dialogue going a bit further beyond what appears to be a short-term fix.

Good leaders are also good followers

General Colin Powell (along with others) used a popular maxim that states, "Take care of the people, and the people will take care of you."[5]

Even though she was a leader in the MJC2 herself, Kayla tried hard to support Gregory. The alpha ape had been a nurturing and supportive boss to her so she tried to reciprocate by being a worthy deputy. Good followership is important for any leader. We all have a boss that we are accountable to in some capacity. Unfortunately, we often do not spend the same amount of energy and focus in managing up as we do managing down.

When Charles asked Kayla what made a good deputy, she surprised the chimpanzee with her response. "Gregory has taught me that being a good leader does not always mean needing to be out in front. Gregory leads by example in this area."

Kayla summed up Gregory's philosophy with the LISTEN acronym:

> A good leader Learns from others while Instilling pride of ownership by Sharing the center stage with others so Teamwork is promoted through keeping one's Ego in check to allow New ideas to be created.

By listening, a leader is not talking, sometimes a good thing.

Followers should protect their gorillas

Kayla shared a poignant story with Charles from Gregory's past involving his father's demise involving another gorilla. As Kayla noted, "Charles, when two large gorillas fight for real, someone is going to get hurt." Gregory's father tangled with a gorilla who did not back down, and in the end, both of them met their premature death.

---

[5] Charles P. Garcia, *Leadership Lessons of the White House Fellows: Learn How to Inspire Others, Achieve Greatness, and Find Success in any Organization* (New York: McGraw-Hill, 2009), 112.

As followers, we need to protect our bosses. Avoid the temptation to send them into battle with other senior leaders (gorillas) for them to fight your pet causes or peeves. Be extra cautious not to egg on your boss with phrases like, "Boy, I cannot believe he made that decision without at least coordinating with you first." Similarly, the following statement waves a red flag in front of a bull, "She always tends to get in your lane. I do not know how you can take it. I know I wouldn't."

As Gregory has demonstrated, collaborating with others to find common ground is going to be more productive than needless confrontation.

Leaders need to manage their ego (as one manages cholesterol)

Referring back to the story of Gregory's father, Kayla shared the following with Charles: "Perhaps you can see now why Gregory tries to keep his emotions and ego in check. He knows it runs through his blood from his father, but he will not follow his father's destructive behavior."

Having ego is like having cholesterol. Two types flow through our veins. The good cholesterol, high-density lipoprotein (HDL) seems to carry cholesterol away from the arteries and back to the liver where it can be passed from the body, thus reducing the risk of heart disease.[6]

Conversely, too much low-density lipoprotein (LDL) is not a good thing because this form of bad cholesterol can build up slowly in the inner walls of the arteries that feed the heart and brain. This potentially forms plaque that narrows the arteries and could lead to a clot that blocks a narrowed artery. A heart attack or stroke can be the result.[7]

Similar to managing cholesterol, a leader must manage his or her ego. Some form of ego may actually be useful and good for us. However, as we saw with Gregory's father, bad ego can be harmful to us if not kept in check.

---

[6] American Heart Association, http://www.americanheart.org.
[7] Ibid.

What is on the inside is more important than the outside

From the very beginning, the Learning Center fascinated Charles. The chimpanzee marveled at the physical magnitude of the building from the outside. Only after Professor Gaylord's tour did he appreciate what was happening inside the construction project.

In the same manner, the inner core of a person, character, is more important than visible attributes. Former Secretary of Defense Robert Gates told a graduating class at the US Naval Academy the following advice:

> Nowadays it seems like integrity—or honor or character—is kind of quaint, a curious, old-fashioned notion ... But for a real leader, personal virtues—self-reliance, self-control, honor, truthfulness, morality—are absolute. These are the building blocks of character, of integrity—and only on that foundation can real leadership be built.[8]

Like it or not, a leader is in a spotlight for others to judge actions as well as words. As the alpha ape, the whole community was aware of Gregory's whereabouts and deeds. In his case, the North Forest populace held him in high esteem because he was a compassionate and caring leader. Consider a situation where you saw a leader fail by ethical or moral failures, not incompetence. As a leader, do not impair your influence and authority through negative activities.

---

[8] *Washington Post*, The Fed Page, May 30, 2011.

CHAPTER FOURTEEN

Time to Ape Up

> After a moment, Gil finally lowered his gaze from
> Gregory and down to the floor. Each second
> that went by seemed like an eternity.

As Gregory climbed up to the branch chief's office, he could hear a conversation going on between Gil and another ape. As he stopped at the doorway, Gregory found Gil and Gabe sitting at the conference table, reviewing what Gregory could only assume were tree-cutting plans.

Not voicing his habitual entrance greeting, Gregory stood silently. Gil either felt his presence or noticed that the room had gone darker because the mammoth ape covered the sunlight. Either way, he turned toward Gregory.

"Gregory, what brings you to visit us baboons?" Gil asked but not in the customary fashion. He reasoned that, if Gregory had not initiated their long-standing greeting, something must be amiss. "Gabe, we can continue this later. I will come and get you after Gregory and I are through. Thanks for your help on this," Gil told the upstart ape.

"Excuse me, sir," Gabe said apologetically as he waited for Gregory to move from the doorway.

The look on Gregory's face was solemn, and Gabe knew better than to continue the playful banter from their earlier time in the work yard.

Gregory offered a half-smile as he stepped aside. "Tell Guy that I look forward to seeing him in that purple dress." He touched the younger ape on his shoulder as he walked through the door. As Gabe began climbing down, he looked up and said, "Yes, sir. Will do."

With that, Gregory turned back toward Gil. Gil had stood up from his spot at the conference room table and waited in awkward silence as Gregory slowly approached him. He had a hunch what this was about, but he chose to let it play out.

Looking Gil squarely in the face, Gregory said, "Kayla provided me an update on the Self-Review Program this afternoon." Quick not to make his deputy the focus of the conversation, Gregory said slowly, "Since the program responses are due tomorrow, I wanted to know if everything were on track."

Gil continued looking at Gregory at eye level, not speaking a word.

Gregory waited a few moments. "The only manager who apparently is not going to meet the deadline is you, Gil. I came here to hear directly from you what is going on."

After a moment, Gil finally lowered his gaze from Gregory and down to the floor. Each second that went by seemed like an eternity. Finally, he looked up and spoke to his old friend. "I am sure that Kayla also told you what I said about the self-review initiative."

Gregory remained motionless and continued staring at Gil.

Noticing Gregory's earlier comment, Gil said, "This has nothing to do with Kayla. Obviously, it is my responsibility to finish the project on time."

Gregory again did not respond, either verbally or nonverbally.

After more tense quietness, Gil spoke, "I was not being truthful to Kayla when I said the self-review was a waste of time and an overreaction to Dawson's accident. I do not believe that at all, Gregory. I know you are especially mindful about the impact on Dawson and his family. Believe it or not, I think it bothers me more."

Gil put his large hand on his silver beard while looking at a distance through the open window to his left. "I think about it every day and sometimes at night in my dreams. Dawson is a good gorilla, straight as can be. I am not sure if he, Bethany, Grover, and Galileo will ever have a normal life again. Not just Dawson's job, but can he ever be a father that is able to play with his brood and teach them to protect themselves and be strong apes?" Shaking his mighty head, Gil said softly, "I am the one who should have ensured that the equipment worked and the apes had the proper safety training." Looking back at his friend and boss, he said, "Me, Gregory. Me."

Softening his expression a bit, Gregory scrunched his face to show his perplexed feeling. He then queried Gil, "If that is true—and I believe you because I feel the same way—then why would you not come up with the self-review questions so it doesn't happen again?"

Gil moved slightly toward Gregory with his arms and hands pointed out. He paused a moment before speaking. "Gregory, you were always the one with the smarts in the group. You could move mountains, but you could also think with your brain. I am not that fortunate. The only reason I am even here is because I could knock down trees and then turn them into buildings. I destroy things, Gregory. And now I have destroyed Dawson's future."

"I am still not following you, Gil. What you are telling me only supports that you believe in the self-review initiative. It is not a waste of time, the way you told Kayla. What am I missing, old friend?"

"I did try, Gregory. I tried to come up with the set of self-review questions that we can use as a checklist on a regular basis. Every day, I would just come up empty. I keep hitting a mental block. It reminds me when I was in school back in the village I came from. Gregory, I was so dumb when it came to writing assignments and papers that I eventually quit high school and decided to move to North Forest. When you needed brute strength instead of a mental giant, I found fulfillment and happiness.

"When you promoted me to branch chief of logistics, I was proud but intimidated at the same time. Why do you think I can barely meet any deadline involving paperwork? I try to blame it on the workload requirements of the tree cutting and maintenance side of things, but in reality, I am a big, dumb ape. I never want to fail you, Gregory. If you need me to step down, maybe it is time that one of the younger and smarter apes takes over. I can go back to the work yard." Gil sighed.

Stunned at the turn of events, Gregory put his large hand on his friend's shoulder and looked at him while Gil's eyes gazed toward the floor.

"Nonsense," Gregory said softly. "The day you go, I will go with you. They will have to throw us both out to pasture with the baboons."

Joseph L. Garcia

Gil laughed and smiled slightly. "I am not sure the baboons will have us."

They both laughed together for a brief second.

"Gil, listen to me. You are one of the best managers in all of Modern Jungle Construction Company. If you do not do your job well, the rest of it doesn't matter. You are a great leader. The younger apes constantly petition me to work in logistics. Even Andreas said so. If I granted all their requests, there would be nobody to work in the rest of the company. They all want to work for Cool School Gil."

Gil walked over to the conference table where he and Gabe were working when Gregory walked in. He looked back at Gregory. "That may be my saving grace. I asked Gabe to help me, and we have already come up with some initial self-review questions. That ape is going to have my job one day."

Walking to the table, Gregory picked up the initial work and reviewed it. "This is right on target. It is a good start, Gil. When do you think you will finish?"

Gil replied, "I could rush it to meet tomorrow's deadline, but I would rather spend a few days to get it right. Probably by Tuesday or Wednesday of next week is more realistic."

Gregory took a deep breath and exhaled. "Gil, I am glad that you have gathered yourself enough to get back in the game. I appreciate your willingness to ape up to your responsibilities. However, do not show up to Monday's staff meeting. I cannot show any favoritism to you or anybody else. The fact is that you should have told Kayla or me what was going on. We could have helped you sooner if you let us. You need to earn your seat at the table. When the other managers ask me where you are at on Monday, I will tell them that you missed an important deadline. That will be your discipline."

Gil looked directly into Gregory's eyes and slowly nodded his head. "I understand, Gregory. Again, I apologize for letting you down."

The alpha ape slowly turned and exited the branch chief's office without saying another word.

CHAPTER FIFTEEN

◆

The Dawson Issue

> "Hannah, in your case, you need to reassess how we determine and use the capabilities of the entire ape force. Ape resources is first and foremost about the ape, not just job benefits or position descriptions."

When Gregory returned to the office, he noticed that Hannah had joined Kayla and Charles and that they were sharing a good laugh. As he sat down in his chair behind the desk, he noticed the drawing of the ape manager and the ape employee on his board.

"Charles, I see that Kayla and Hannah have been going over Ape Management 101 with you." Gregory chuckled as he interlocked his mighty hands behind his head. "When you figure it out, please let me know because I can never keep up with either of them."

Charles was quick to reply. "Actually, Gregory, we've had a very interesting conversation about ape resources and what tends to work well. It seems that good communication is an important key to success."

Gregory nodded his head several times before straightening up in his chair. "You are absolutely right, my friend. Although communication is relatively simple, we can make it more difficult than it has to be. Just talking to your fellow ape to glimpse what is going on in his or her mind can do wonders."

Kayla spoke hesitantly, "So, how did it go with Gil?"

"Fine, fine. He is getting help from Gabe on the self-review questions. He will be a few days late, but I believe his end product will be excellent." Gregory did not feel he should elaborate on the rest of the dialogue between him and Gil, so he changed the subject. "Well, Hannah, what options do we have with Dawson? What did the medical team determine regarding his long-term work prospects?"

The AR manager shook her head slowly while holding Dawson's personnel file. "Not good, Gregory. The doctors do not think he should work in the logistics area again. His back is still strained, and he will likely have pain the rest of his life. Continuing in the work yard is not an option."

Gregory lowered his gaze as he took in the conversation with Hannah. After a moment, he looked at Kayla. "What do we have on the administrative side of the business that Dawson could be cross-trained on? Let me be clear. He will not be laid off because of this accident."

Charles noticed that both Kayla and Hannah seemed nervous for the first time. Gone was the laughter they had enjoyed in the room just moments before Gregory returned.

"Boss, Hannah and I have reviewed Dawson's situation, and we have a couple options to consider."

At that point, both Kayla and Hannah moved to the two chairs in front of Gregory's desk. Charles casually picked up Dawson's personnel file that Hannah had left behind.

Kayla said, "One option is that we place Dawson on some type of disability retirement. That way, we will not risk him being hurt on the job again doing the work he was doing before."

After an instant, it was Hannah's turn to address Gregory. Charles observed that it appeared they had rehearsed this discussion ahead of time.

"The other option is that we place him in administrative support. There are no vacancies right now in AR or procurement. However, we are short an intern or two, so he could help with some of the filing and other duties until we figure something out more permanently."

Charles looked up from Dawson's folder when he noticed that the conversation had gone dead silent. Gregory took a deep breath and then exhaled. Clearly, he did not like the options his deputy and AR chief had presented to him regarding Dawson's intermediate future.

"I know you are only trying to do what is best for Dawson, and I appreciate your research of alternatives. There is much more to it than that. It is hard to explain." Gregory got up and walked to the back window with its view toward the work yard. With the proper angle, he could see the young apes working on the tree cutting or even their occasional horseplay.

"Dawson is a proud gorilla. Like the rest of us males, he has a need to protect and provide for his family." Staring out the window to the lush forest directly behind him, Gregory was deliberate with his choice of words. "Dawson will not be filing paperwork for the next three months or whatever it takes to find him something permanent. He did nothing wrong. If anything, Mighty Jungle Construction Company let him down." Gregory slowly turned around and looked at the two female gorillas. "I am relying on you to come up with something that provides Dawson a paycheck but also gives him meaningful work."

Kayla and Hannah looked at each and nodded their heads. They knew they had their work cut out for them on this one.

"Did you know that Dawson has a business degree from college?" Charles spoke to no one in particular as he read his file.

Hannah replied, "Really? I never realized he even attended college. However, the accounting shop is relatively small, and like Gregory just said, he does not want Dawson doing busy work."

Charles looked up from Dawson's file. "No, I was not thinking about accounting."

Intrigued, Kayla looked at Charles. "Charles, what did you have in mind?"

Charles stood up and left Dawson's file on the couch. "I feel hesitant to bring up anything because I am nothing more than an unworthy visitor who has been given such warmth and hospitality by all of you."

Gregory intervened. "Charles, if there is one thing we believe here, is that any and every ape can make a difference. Please, this is no time for modesty."

Kayla followed suit. "Yes, Hannah and I are stuck. We could use an objective opinion."

"Charles, I totally agree," said Hannah. "What are you thinking?"

Charles started his statement in a deliberate tone. "It occurs to me that we should look for the logical connection that seems to exist right in front of us."

The room was completely quiet as the three large gorillas stared at this diminutive figure in their midst, hanging on to his every word.

Charles said, "If I understand things correctly, the reason that Gregory has been pushing hard for the Self-Review Program in the first place is in response to Dawson's accident." He paused. "Then who better to manage the new Self-Review program than—"

Before Charles could finish his sentence, Gregory clapped his hands together and voiced loudly, "Dawson!"

Charles smiled and nodded his head in agreement.

Gregory put up his hands and addressed Charles, "Sorry, Charles, for interrupting. Please finish your thoughts."

"Well, you figured it out yourself," Charles replied. "With his business degree and background in the operational side of the business, Dawson would be an ideal choice to manage the new Self-Review Program. He would be a living reminder why the program was important in the first place. It seems a new position could be created for him as the self-review manager. He could work directly for Gregory or Kayla. Perhaps even you, Hannah."

"I think Kayla would be the perfect choice if you ask me," replied Hannah.

"Gregory, what do you think?" asked his deputy.

The alpha ape had crossed both arms across his vast chest as he took it all in. "Dawson being the self-review manager is good for another reason. He would serve as a great example of why it is important to stay in school and finish a college degree. Too many apes are leaving school early and going to work in logistics. I also think Dawson working for Kayla would be a good idea." Gregory uncrossed his arms and held his right index finger pointed to the ceiling as if about to say something else.

"However, I believe that Dawson should work for Gil instead."

Charles noticed that Kayla gave a brief look of disappointment, but she quickly recovered. "Boss, tell us what you are thinking."

Gregory looked directly at Kayla. "It goes back to what Charles mentioned earlier about a logical connection right in front of us. The idea of the Self-Review Program started because of Dawson's accident in the first place, right? The supervisor and program most directly connected to the accident, and thus the Self-Review Program is Gil, the logistics branch chief. He feels guilty that the accident occurred on his watch. It would mean a lot to Gil's confidence to be able to work side by side with Dawson to actually roll out the program. Kayla, I am going to need your help to work with Gil. He could use your writing and communication skills. Let him take the lead, but I know that, with your help, the Self-Review Program will be a big success."

Kayla regained her composure. "Of course, Gregory, I will do everything to support both Gil and Dawson. It makes perfect sense."

Gregory walked back to his desk and sat down. Both Kayla and Hannah looked at him silently because it appeared that Gregory had more to say.

"I believe there are several lessons for us to consider. First, it appears that you two had not totally done your homework when it came to Dawson. You were quick to stereotype him as a labor worker, and your two options of early retirement or busy work reflected that assumption. Second, the Self-Review Program is not just about the accident and logistics. It applies to all facets of the Mighty Jungle Construction Company. Hannah, in your case, you need to reassess how we determine and use the capabilities of the entire ape force. Ape resources is first and foremost about the ape, not just job benefits or position descriptions." Gregory looked directly at the two senior manager apes sitting in front of him. "Is that a fair assessment?"

His deputy was the first to answer. "Yes, sir, very fair. I take responsibility for not coming up with viable options for Dawson's situation. We were too quick to come up with a solution without understanding the ape himself." She turned behind her to face Charles. "I want to thank you, Charles, for your recommendations. Your objective viewpoint was most valuable."

The alpha ape peeked around Hannah and Kayla. "Yes, thank you, Charles. Thank you very much for your insight."

Hannah spoke, "I appreciate your willingness to speak up, Charles. I am most grateful." She looked back at Gregory. "You are right about the Self-Review Program, sir. I will get started on developing a full set of issues that warrant a comprehensive review."

A loud double knock on the door frame startled the group as Andreas suddenly appeared.

"Sorry to interrupt, boss." The young male ape grinned.

"Yes, Andreas, what is it?" Gregory replied.

The assistant proudly proclaimed, "Everything is set for this afternoon, sir. There was no problem whatsoever with the change."

Before anybody could inquire as to what had changed in the first place, Gregory walked over to Charles. "Charles, how would you like to come with me to work out at the fitness center? I want you to see the facility before you leave."

CHAPTER SIXTEEN

◆

Pumping Wood

> The noise got so loud that apes walking on the trail outside could hear the commotion and turned inquisitively toward the fitness center.

G regory left his deputy and the AR manager back in the office to finish the details regarding Dawson. He instructed them to run it by Dawson immediately to see if he were interested. However, Gregory wanted a private meeting arranged in the morning to ensure that Dawson had no reservations about the new position.

As Charles walked with the alpha ape toward the gym, he began to have conflicting thoughts. On the one hand, he missed Taylor specifically and South Forest generally. It had been nearly twenty-four hours since he had left the meeting with Cyrus, but it seemed much longer. Here, he felt at ease and welcome among the gorillas. As Charles looked up at Gregory, he realized he was going to miss his new friend.

Because Gregory was not one to make small talk while they walked, Charles felt comfortable just taking in the enormous complex from this western view. He enjoyed walking on the trail that connected the major venues of the compound. To his immediate left, he could see Gil's branch chief office, which stood out because it was the only one located in a tree. Directly behind it was the large work yard where Charles could see the crews performing their various tree-splitting functions.

As the trail turned in a northerly direction, Charles noticed on his left the library and a hospital. Surprisingly, they were not on multiple levels like the Learning Center but housed on a single floor. At this point, the pair was located at the extreme western side. Charles looked to his right to see the enormous amphitheater on the far eastern side of the complex. From this view, it was magnificent with the large stage and columns placed on both sides. Charles could see why Gregory had proudly called it his favorite part of the community earlier in the day.

Gregory looked down at Charles who was lagging behind a bit so he could take in the panoramic views of North Forest. His diminutive visitor was clearly engrossed in watching the various structures all around him.

Gregory knew their time was soon ending and Charles would need to return to South Forest and resume his own responsibilities as business chimp and husband. Gregory felt a strange peace around the chimpanzee and was sad that he may not ever see him again.

"Gregory, I heard you were bringing a special guest with you today. This strapping chimpanzee must be the one and only Charles." The personal trainer gave a slight bow to both of them. He had walked outside the fitness center to meet them while both Gregory and Charles were deep in their private thoughts.

"Charles, I would like you to meet Brayson. He runs the fitness center and is also my personal tormenter … uh, I mean trainer. Brayson, this, as you already have observed, is Charles."

"Pleasure to meet you," Charles said to the well-built ape.

As Brayson straightened up, he waved them through the front opening of the gym. "Please, come on in. Everything is ready."

Charles marveled at how spacious the facility was on the inside. The front view from off the trail did not do it justice. To his immediate left was a tree-climbing area that Charles noticed was set up for training younger apes. In front of him was another area with an instructor leading a group of gorillas through stretching and breathing exercises.

Charles continued to follow Gregory and Brayson while taking in other parts of the fitness center. Judging by the number of gorillas and the various activities, Charles reasoned that this was a popular spot in the compound.

Brayson led them through a door, and when Charles entered the large room, he was impressed with what he saw. Many gorillas were lifting what appeared to be various cuts of trees. Charles surmised that, because they were completely stripped bare, they came from the work yard.

Charles thought, *This must be the strength room.*

Charles recognized several of the apes who were working out intensely. Nathan, the ape from the fire station cistern near the Learning Center, was curling a thick branch that had two equally sized trunks on both sides. The tree trunks had a hole in the middle that allowed them to fit over each end.

Close to him was Guy, the ape who promised to wear a purple outfit so others could see him in the Tree Run through the Forest competition. He was lifting a similar contraption, although the branch and trunks were thicker and larger, up above his head and back to his shoulders.

In the middle of the room, prominently displayed were seven, evenly spaced stations. Each had a large, wooden base that served as a bench for the gorillas to lay flat. Again, all the wood was completely stripped bare of any bark or even a single leaf.

Two enormous trunks of equal height and size surrounded each bench. The middle portions were cut hollow about one foot, allowing a sizeable tree branch to fit in between both trunks. Judging by the size of the horizontal branches, the weight of each station grew progressively larger from left to right. Charles then noticed the sign at the first station said "Three Hundred Pounds" and increased incrementally by a hundred pounds until reaching nine hundred pounds on the far right. Most of the middle stations were occupied as the gorillas pressed close to their body weight, depending on their maturity and size.

Brayson approached Charles and whispered to him, "Gregory will start at the nine hundred-pound station to warm up. Then we will go to a private room that is set up just for him. Actually, him and Gil. They are the only two who can lift twelve hundred pounds. For that weight, I need to help him clear the large branch over the top of the tree trunks."

As Gregory began easily lifting the massive weight in smooth repetitions, Brayson leaned over to Charles. "In the other room, I have set up some smaller weights that I think you can handle. Gregory thought you would like to try them without all the other apes around. Don't worry. I will be close by to assist in case you get stuck."

Charles looked up at Brayson, who was smiling down at him. The chimpanzee began walking slowly to the vacant station on the left, the one marked "Three Hundred Pounds."

"Charles, no, not that one. I have yours set up in the backroom." Brayson started after Charles.

Gregory, who had finished his warm-up presses, came over to see what was going on. The trainer apologetically told the alpha ape, "Gregory, I am not sure what your visitor is trying to do. I told him that you wanted his workout in the private room."

Gregory turned to the chimpanzee. "Charles, I have to go along with Brayson. You might get hurt trying to lift that branch. It may not look like it, but it really weighs three hundred pounds, like the sign says."

Charles looked at both of them and quietly stated, "Trust me. I got this. Please do not make a big deal out of it."

As he stretched out on his back, he noticed Gregory motioning for Brayson to stand over the thick branch to assist Charles when he needed it. Charles simply nodded his head in disapproval. Gregory reluctantly called off Brayson away from behind the press station.

Although diminutive in size compared to his massive gorilla cousins, Charles weighed approximately 150 pounds. As he began to prepare himself mentally for the lifts, he recalled the strength sessions from his college football days. They did not involve large tree branches and tree trunks, but actually lifting other chimps. It was a number of years ago, but as fullback, he was one of the strongest chimps on the team.

The fitness center grew quiet as the gorillas working out began noticing what was happening. They stopped their routines and gathered slowly around the scene, respecting the space as to not crowd too close to Charles. A nervous Gregory inched forward as much as he could without offending Charles. If necessary, he wanted to be close enough to grab the thick branch before it fell down on his newfound friend. All eyes were on Charles, who appeared to be ready to attempt the initial lift. Gregory noticed that Charles had long, strong arms that would allow him to grasp the branch without any assistance.

There was complete silence in the strength room. Charles easily cleared the first step, pressing the heavy branch out of the middle grooves straight upward until both of his arms were upright. Then he began to lower the thick branch slowly to his chest.

As he pushed up again to the starting position, Nathan interrupted the silence with a drawn out "One." Charles held the position for a brief second while moving his fingers on the branch. Gregory instinctively raised both arms at shoulder level in case he needed to rush in. In reality, the chimpanzee was getting used to the odd grip of bare wood.

Down went the thick branch again to his chest as Charles then lifted it up a second time.

"Two," said Nathan with a bit more confidence in his count.

Charles now felt in a groove with the grip and weight as he began smooth and clean repetitions.

Soon, other apes began to join in the count, "Three ... four ... five ... six ... seven." A few started shouting out words of encouragement, "Come on, Charles. You can do it!" Still another yelled, "Keep going, Charles! You got a lot left in you!" The chimpanzee, lifting twice his body mass, continued in a steady fashion.

When he hit fifteen reps, however, Charles began to feel the weight taking its toll. He had mentally set a goal of twenty presses, and he felt that it would be close. The gorillas around Charles were now in full support and holding nothing back with their loud encouragement. Some were beating their chests, and still others hunched over, pounding on the floor. The noise got so loud that apes walking on the trail outside could hear the commotion and turned inquisitively toward the fitness center.

Charles had slowed considerably, but when he reached eighteen presses, he thought to himself, *Only two more to go.*

Gregory was no longer worried about his friend's ability to handle the weight, and his concern had turned to awe at what he was seeing. He had clearly underestimated a chimpanzee's strength.

The frenzy continued as the gorillas knew instinctively that Charles was aiming for twenty presses.

As Charles began to press up number nineteen, the gorilla group grew respectfully quiet as they held their breath for their comrade.

When he fully extended his arms, mighty cheers and more chest thumping broke the silence.

Charles took three deep breaths while holding the increasingly heavy branch. He began to slowly lower the branch toward his chest, but he knew that was the easy part. Getting it back up one final time would be the challenge.

This time, all the gorillas in the strength room, even Gregory, began shouting in unison, compelling Charles to complete the last lift. Slowly, the branch moved upward, an inch per second. By the look on his grimaced face, everyone knew that this was all that Charles had in him.

Finally, he was able to lock his arms vertically as the gorillas yelled, "Twenty!"

Charles still needed to muster the strength to return the branch between the two trunks, but he did so without a problem. As he returned to an upright position on the bench, the gorillas loudly applauded his efforts. They parted as he began to walk toward Gregory and Brayson.

The alpha ape was the first to speak, "Charles, I knew you were an extremely intelligent chimp, but I had no idea that you were a super strong one too. I owe you an apology. I was too quick to judge you by your size. I just told Hannah and Kayla not to stereotype apes, and here I did exactly the same thing. Can you forgive me?"

Charles looked up smiling, nearly out of breath, and said, "Gregory, all I want you to do is promise me, if I ever try something like that again, you stop me."

Gregory laughed. "Are you kidding? The next time, I expect you to try the nine hundred-pound station."

He put his arm around the tired chimp as they both followed Brayson into the private room. Before entering, Charles looked back one more time to see the primate pandemonium that continued in the strength room.

◆

CHAPTER SEVENTEEN

Winding Down

Gregory saw Charles observing the falling sun and finally spoke up, "Charles, I know you will want to be heading back to South Forest soon, but there is one surprise left to show you if you are up to it."

"Charles, wake up. It is time to get moving."

"No, Taylor, let me sleep five more minutes."

A deep voice followed a firm push. "I am not Taylor, and no, you cannot sleep five more minutes."

Charles slowly opened his eyes to see a large face that did not resemble Taylor's at all. It was Gregory. As Charles sat up on the bench, he rubbed his eyes with both his hands and tried to reorient his bearings. He remembered doing some stretching exercises in the private room while Gregory did his own strength routine. Afterward, they took a dip in the fire station cistern in the back of the facility and then lay out on the outside benches. Charles must have fallen asleep.

As he rubbed his shoulders, Charles could feel the soreness beginning to develop from his earlier presses in the strength room. Although he was stiff, he smiled as he recollected the way he had surprised everyone with his twenty repetitions at the three hundred-pound station.

"Friend, the swim really relaxed you. That and the afternoon sun put you out like a lion after a good meal," Gregory said.

Charles, fully awake now, looked over at the alpha ape. "Gregory, how do you do it? The workout, nice dip, and then a nap. They were great, but how do you find the time to be away from the job for so long? I could never do that."

Gregory replied, "The better question Charles is this. How do you not do it?"

"What do you mean?"

"You just said that the exercise and rest felt great, so why would you not do something that feels great? Work is work, and non-work is non-work. You have to find a balance that works for you. Edna told me that she likes to chase the crocodiles by the river for relaxation."

Charles could only imagine a mammoth elephant stomping through the water and creating havoc with the predators waiting patiently to seize a prey.

"Besides," Gregory said, "Kayla can tend to any business that comes up while I'm not in the office. If something were really an emergency, she knows where to find me. Trust me. That rarely happens."

Charles took in what Gregory was telling him. By not exercising and getting the proper rest and relaxation, he actually had less energy, both mental and physical. While looking at Gregory, the chimp noticed the sun beneath him beginning to set behind them. He had to admit that even the sunsets seemed more calm and peaceful in North Forest.

Gregory saw Charles observing the falling sun and finally spoke up. "Charles, I know you will want to be heading back to South Forest soon, but there is one surprise left to show you if you are up to it."

Although he was anxious to return home, Charles reasoned that one more sight to see or place to visit would be a fitting end to a magnificent day. "Of course. I look forward to what you have in mind, my friend."

"Good. Follow me," was all that Gregory said as they left the back of the fitness center, headed to the walking trail in front, and traveled in a northerly direction.

As they walked along the trail, Charles could see the mayor's office to his left. Directly behind it was the Modern Jungle Construction Company—Administrative Offices where Gregory had met with the union while Charles visited with Kayla. When the trail straightened toward the east, Charles could see a few gorillas heading to the Learning

Center. In fact, for the first time, he noticed very few apes were on the walking trail at that precise moment.

Charles finally broke the silence. "Gregory, the compound seems unnaturally quiet and without much activity going on. The few apes I do see appear to be going toward the Learning Center. Is Professor Gaylord giving a special lecture of some kind? Is that the surprise you mentioned?"

Gregory smiled and looked downward to the visitor walking to his right. "It took me all day, but I think I have finally stumped you, Charles. Your logic is sound because the apes up ahead are technically heading toward the Learning Center. However, you will see in a second that they are going to walk past it and continue toward the amphitheater. That is the surprise. I asked Andreas to arrange with the North Forest Arts Society for the Thursday afternoon practice to turn into an impromptu performance. I wanted you to see our youth ensemble perform. They were scheduled tomorrow for our weekly Friday afternoon event."

Charles looked up at Gregory and with his mouth slightly open before speaking. "I do not know what to say, Gregory. I do not deserve this gesture or any of the special acts of generosity and kindness that you have shown me today. I just barged into North Forest, and instead of treating me as a trespasser, you have rolled out the red carpet. I never meant to take up your valuable time and that of the community."

Gregory looked down at the chimpanzee as they continued walking. "We are the ones who benefited from your wit, inquisitive nature, and wisdom." Feeling a need to change the mood as they neared the amphitheater entrance, the gorilla laughed. "And besides, you are so strong that, if we do not treat you right, you might beat us up!"

As they came up closer to the massive venue on their right, Charles could hear the audience on the other side of the large dirt wall facing him. When they got near the northern entrance into the amphitheater, Gregory stopped so Charles could proceed through first.

The moment that Charles walked through the archway, the large crowd burst into a loud applause. At first, Charles thought the crowd was recognizing Gregory, whom he assumed was directly behind him.

In the middle of the commotion, he heard his name being called from slightly to his left. "Charles, Charles, over here."

It was Kayla and Hannah, who were sitting in the front row closest to the stage. When he turned to speak to Gregory, the alpha ape was nowhere to be found. Charles looked up on stage, thinking that perhaps Gregory was going to speak to the large gathering, but only younger apes were gathered.

While approaching the front row, Hannah noticed that Charles appeared to be looking for Gregory. She discretely pointed to the back of the amphitheater. Charles turned to notice that Gregory had walked all the way toward the last row and Gil was standing to greet him. When the alpha ape approached, he paused and then slowly raised his right hand, knuckles facing outward. Gil did the same until both of their knuckles grazed the other for a moment.

When he took his seat between Kayla and Hannah, he asked both of them, "Why is Gregory sitting so far back? I thought he would join us here."

The deputy spoke first. "Gregory never sits up front. He says it is because he and Gil are so big that no one could see over them. In reality, it just shows that Gregory is a humble leader who does not want any special treatment. When we tried to follow his example, he insisted we should represent Mighty Jungle with the rest of the community."

A gorilla sitting behind them leaned forward and offered another perspective. "Gregory once told me that he likes to sit in the farthest row back because that way he can see the entire stage in front of him. If he is too close, he misses things."

Hannah began to make the introductions. "Dawson, I want you to meet—"

And before she could finish, he said, "Charles, of course. I want to thank you for coming up with the idea of making me the self-review manager for the company. My wife Bethany here and I are very grateful."

Charles noticed the smiling female gorilla sitting next to him. "Actually, Kayla and Hannah made everything happen. I just happened to make an observation, and they jumped in to finish up the details," Charles said modestly and turned to Bethany. "Where are your boys, Grover and Galileo? I met them earlier with Gregory, and they are very polite and well mannered. You should be proud of them."

Bethany replied, "Thank you, Charles. They are up on the stage. You see them? They are in the middle row."

Before Charles could answer, the conductor began to tap his stick on a wooden pedestal in the center of the stage. "North Forest community," the gorilla said loudly, "at Gregory's request." He then motioned to the back where the alpha ape was sitting. "We are conducting an impromptu performance this afternoon in honor of our visitor from South Forest, Mr. Charles."

Kayla motioned for Charles to stand on the wooden row so the community could see him. Reluctantly, the chimpanzee did so and waved his arms to the audience around him.

As the applause continued, Charles took in the magnificent structure that Gregory was so proud of himself. It appeared that the gorillas had created the seating part of the venue by moving a great amount of dirt. They moved the earth from the middle area to create a wall that formed a sort of semicircle behind him.

The northern wall to his right continued from the back all the way to the stage. They created a wide tunnel that led into the seating area. To his left, the southern wall, for some reason, came only halfway toward the stage. To the immediate right and left of the raised stage were large column figures. The apes must have dug deep holes to anchor them properly because they were perfectly straight. Directly in front was a large, rectangular water cistern. This cistern, unlike the others, was lower and more decorative to blend into the amphitheater décor.

Genius, Charles thought.

When the applause died down, Charles returned to his sitting position. He felt embarrassed with all the attention. Strangely, he also felt disconnected not being near Gregory, his companion for most of the day. He looked back to see Gil and Gregory in conversation.

When things settled down, the performance began. The youth ensemble sang songs, some individual apes read poetry, and there was even choreographed dancing. When Grover and Galileo sang a duet, Charles turned back to Dawson and Bethany to offer his congratulations.

After the last act, the audience gave a rousing ovation. Charles turned around to see Gregory and Gil clapping loudly and shouting encouragement to the young performers. Behind the mammoth pair, Charles noticed that the sun was nearly even with the horizon.

It will be dark soon, Charles thought.

After saying his good-byes to Kayla, Hannah, Dawson, and Bethany, other apes came by to bid him farewell. He recognized most from various locations. A few introduced themselves for the first time.

The venue was near empty when Gregory came by with Gil.

The branch chief spoke first, "Charles, it was a great pleasure to meet you today, and I hope to see you again soon. You are always welcome in North Forest."

Charles looked up and nodded his head before speaking. "Thank you, Gil. I would like to see you again too."

Gregory led Charles toward the southern exit of the amphitheater.

Before leaving, Charles asked Gregory, "Why is the southern wall incomplete?"

Gregory smiled. "This southern side is partially open to allow the elephants enough room to enter the amphitheater and put out a fire on the large stage."

Charles shook his head. "I should have figured that one out."

"You've had a long day, Charles. You are entitled to one miss." Gregory chuckled.

As they walked away from the amphitheater, the pair left the trail that connected all the major venues of the community. They walked in silence, but this time, it felt different to Charles. This interlude felt awkward as if both wanted to say something, but neither wanted to be the first to do so.

After a little while, Charles could see the pool where he refreshed himself and first met Gregory. It was hard to believe that he had experienced so much since their morning encounter.

When he dipped down for a drink, he noticed some movement off in the distance.

He looked up at Gregory. "I see a pair of large gorillas trying to hide behind that tree. What are they up to or—should I say—what are you up to, Gregory?"

"Your eyesight is excellent, Mr. Chimp Executive Officer. Those two, on the other hand, could use some lessons on hiding in the jungle. You got me, Charles. Nathan and Gabe volunteered to shadow you back to your village when they heard you were going to stay for the afternoon concert." The alpha ape grumbled. "Some shadows, you already spotted them before taking one step on your return journey."

"I promise I will not let on." Charles half-laughed.

Gregory took a deep breath. "Charles, I am not very good at saying good-bye, so this may get clumsy."

The chimp looked up. "I know what you mean."

"I enjoyed our time together, Charles. I never had a brother growing up ... it is a long story ... but somehow I view you as more than a new friend. I learned a lot from you today."

Charles replied, "I was the student today. I cannot tell you how much I've tried to take in from all the experiences of the day. Thank you for graciously allowing me to be a bystander. My only regret is that I did not write down some of my observations so I could remember them when I get back. I will never be able to recollect all the key lessons."

Gregory paused for a moment and then looked around. He found a twig and then returned to where Charles was standing. "Charles, you realize that gorillas and chimpanzees may be different in size, but we come from the same ape family." Gregory leaned over and began writing on the ground near the pool. When he was finished, he spoke softly to Charles, "A simple way I remember how to lead is APE."

Charles leaned over to see what the alpha ape had written on the ground.

Accountable

Partner

Everyone

Gregory gave Charles a moment before proceeding. "I am accountable for my actions. It starts with me to do the right thing. Never go it alone. Always partner with others. Finally, everyone is important and can make a difference. You see. APE," said Gregory.

Charles stood staring at the simple but powerful philosophy that his new friend had shared with him. "That makes sense to me. Perfect sense." He nodded his head. The day's events flashed in his mind:

- Gregory held himself accountable for Dawson's accident
- Gil held accountable for missing the self-review deadline
- Kayla and Hannah for poor analysis of Dawson's options
- Partnering with the union to keep apes in college

- Gregory partnering with Edna and the elephants for tree cutting that was good for them and the environment
- Partnering with the mayor to form a committee that led to the fire response cisterns strategically located in the compound
- Everyone is important.

The list included Andreas, Dawson, Kayla, Hannah, the younger apes he inspired in the work yard, and even a visitor like myself, thought Charles

Gregory interrupted him. "You'd better get going, Charles. It will be dark soon, and the jungle can be a dangerous place at nighttime."

Charles walked toward the invisible boundary that separated North Forest from South Forest.

Gregory said, "You're a good ape, Charles."

Charles turned slowly toward the jungle and began walking when he heard, "Wait."

"I take that back," Gregory said curtly.

As Charles turned around, he felt a pang of disappointment. *Is this going to be a Cyrus moment, where his boss gives an awkward acknowledgement of praise?*

"I take that back," Gregory said. "You are not a good ape, Charles." He paused. "You are a great ape." As he said the words, the alpha ape extended his right hand with his knuckles out.

Charles looked at the large hand and then at his brother ape's face that seemed to be holding back a tear. He slowly raised his right hand, knuckles facing out, and grazed Gregory's outstretched hand.

Then for the first time—and what would likely be the last time—the large ape and small ape hugged each other.

DEVELOPING YOUR
GORILLA QUOTIENT (GQ):
FOURTH REFLECTION

Stereotyping followers limits your ability to lead them

Too often, leaders will sell their followers short when it comes to challenging them to achieve great things. Instead of stretching their followers with new targets and objectives, a leader can set the bar too low. In essence, followers will rise (or fall) to the leader's expectation.

Kayla and Hannah stereotyped Dawson as a work yard laborer, and as a result, they offered less than optimal solutions for Gregory to consider. In their minds, an injured, blue-collar gorilla was not going to add much value outside of the logistics area. Their options included taking him out of the workforce completely (early retirement) or doing administrative busy work (filing).

It took Charles' fresh set of eyes to look at Dawson differently. He was an educated ape that could jump-start the Self-Review Program that Gregory was so anxious to implement.

Surprisingly, the lion chaser was later guilty of stereotyping Charles because of a visible image of him. To a seven hundred-pound gorilla, an ape that was approximately one-fifth his size could not possibly be physically strong.

After all, Charles was obviously an intellectual ape because of his CEO position and the many insightful questions he raised. Gregory relayed to Brayson (his trainer) that the chimpanzee should not be embarrassed by lifting weights in front of the stronger gorillas. Instead of maximizing his opportunities, Gregory was minimizing them by giving him smaller weights. Avoid any stereotyping.

A "total" leader leads all people

Despite his misjudgment of Charles' strength in the weight room (which he later apologized to his chimpanzee visitor), we observe that what makes Gregory a special leader is his willingness to engage each and all members of the workforce: Dawson, the injured ape; his friend and branch chief, Gil; the young apes in the work yard; and Kayla and Hanna as his deputy and HR manager, respectively. All of them mattered to Gregory.

We often hear the term "complete" or "total" used when referring to someone who has mastered a certain skill. Pete Rose once called San Francisco Giant Juan Marichal "the most complete pitcher" because, while in a jam, he could throw any one of five pitches for a strike.[9] A total piano player has a reputation for excellence in rhythm and pace and has a good ear for the accompanying music.

You cannot consider yourself a complete leader, a total leader, if you are not leading all of your people. If someone's talent is left behind, you are not maximizing your organizational performance. You must lead everyone in your unit, not just the ones you like. If any person is not fully participating, then he or she is not fully contributing. If someone is not abundantly adding value, you are going to come up short in meeting your own mission. Your organization's performance will be less than 100 percent.

If a leader excludes anyone from participating and contributing for whatever reason, the mission will suffer. Look at the impact of President Lincoln's decision to allow African American soldiers into the Civil War fight. He noted in August 1864, "Take away from us and give the enemy the hundred and thirty, forty, or fifty thousand colored persons now us as soldiers, seaman, and laborers and we cannot longer maintain the contest."[10]

---

[9]   Wayne Stewart, *The Gigantic Book of Baseball Quotations* (New York: Skyhorse Publishing, 2007), 231.

[10] The Lincoln Institute Presents, *Mr. Lincoln and Freedom*, http://www. mrlincolnandfreedom.org, 05/14/2014

In a similar manner, my active duty experience on 9/11 taught me a valuable lesson regarding the importance of everyone contributing to the fight. I was stationed at the Pentagon at the time, working for the Office of Air Force Reserve.

On that fateful morning, I was proceeding to our command section on the other side of the Pentagon, where I ran into my boss. He asked me if I had heard what had just occurred in New York City, and I told him that I had not. We stepped into the nearby public affairs office that had a television set on and started watching the horrific news unfold. After what seemed only a few minutes, we heard and slightly felt a thud at the Pentagon, one of the largest office buildings in the world. The time was 9:38 a.m., Eastern Standard Time.

We immediately turned to our left, and because we were on the highest floor (fifth) and there were windows to look through, we saw the flames and black smoke coming directly from the opposite side of the building. We did not know it at the time, but it was Flight 77. The flames and smoke were going over the roof from the crash site.

After the 9/11 attacks, I had an increased exposure to the many reservists and guardsmen called to fight and defend our country. Previously, many of us on active duty stereotyped this group as "weekend warriors." Imagine if our senior leadership did not use the guard or reserve forces because they felt they were different somehow.

I gained a tremendous respect for their commitment, dedication, and performance. The same holds true today for all our brave reservists and guardsmen in all military branches who have taken the fight to our enemies. Many served multiple tours in tough combat conditions. Fortunately, we as a nation have gained a greater appreciation of their contributions to our national defense as part of the total force.

Never stereotype others of different physical characteristics, race, creed, religion, age, and gender. If any person or group is held back and has a glass ceiling imposed on him or her, then you also have a glass ceiling on your ability to meet your mission as a leader.

A team cannot be a total or complete team if you do not allow everyone in it. In the same manner, you cannot be a total or complete leader until you are leading the entire team.

Epilogue: One Year Later

The young assistant turned to greet his boss when he noticed him walking through the door. "Good morning, sir. I've got a fresh pot of coconut juice going."

"Thanks, Andreas. That sounds good. I do love your coconut juice." As Andreas poured the brew, he said, "Gregory called this morning. He said everything is set and he looks forward to your arrival. Your deputy is waiting for you in the conference room, sir. I think she is more excited than you are about today."

Upon entering the conference room, Ravae greeted him warmly. "Good morning, Charles. I thought we may want to practice your lines one more time before the big ceremony."

Charles had promoted his former special assistant to deputy CEO shortly after his visit to North Forest. Gregory had graciously arranged for Ravae to shadow Kayla for a week to get a better feel for a deputy's role.

When Ravae moved up, Charles offered Andreas the position of special assistant. The energetic ape quickly accepted. He became the first gorilla to move to South Forest, and the chimpanzee community greeted him warmly. Charles had granted Andreas his longing to see new sights and do different things.

"Charles, how can you not be bouncing off the walls? This is such a big event for our communities," Ravae proclaimed.

"I will leave the bouncing off walls to Cliff," Charles bemused.

Inside, he had to admit he was very excited about today's significant ceremony. The past year had been phenomenal on several fronts. Charles and CHIMP Inc. had expanded the Virtual Vine concept across all of South Forest and then recently added North Forest. Cliff and Autumn added a Forest Code—one for South Forest and two for North

Forest—that allowed the original configuration to be used with only slight modification.

Gregory and Mighty Jungle Construction Company had signed a long-term agreement with South Forest to begin development of a hospital, a new Learning Center, and, at Charles' insistence, a fully equipped fitness center.

He took Gregory's advice and now delegated many tasks to Ravae. In the meantime, he could visit Brayson, who had become his personal trainer, three times a week in the North Forest fitness center.

During the interim building period, all chimpanzees were welcome to use any of the North Forest facilities. Professor Gaylord at the Learning Center graciously offered to integrate chimps into all of the grades through high school.

In order to facilitate travel between the two communities, Gregory and MJC2 had established a treetop shuttle service. They constructed a gondola lift using intertwined branches and vines that could carry up to four chimps at a time. Using simple gravity, the gondolas needed a descent of only a few inches across the entire trip to reach the other side. To return home, travelers used a similar arrangement on a separate route.

Because the trees on both ends were extremely tall, a separate lift hoisted up infants, the elderly, or chimpanzees with special needs. Gorillas were on both ends of the shuttle service on a weeklong detail from Gil's logistics branch.

In reality, the young apes enjoyed the break from the tree-cutting duties, and the female chimps always fawned over the gorillas' strength. Gil had to intervene for them to tone it down with their muscle posing because it was causing a problem among the male chimps. He asked Hannah to purchase large and baggy company shirts to cover their brawny physiques. The young apes were not fond of the idea at first but helped design the MJC2 shirt logo.

Edna arranged for young elephants to provide free elephant taxi rides for gorillas on the lift crews or when Gregory or others conducted business in South Forest. Again, it offered a work diversion for the elephants who volunteered, and Edna saw it as a way to keep the younger herd members in shape.

Ravae interrupted. "Charles, do you have your lines memorized? We can go over them one more time if you would like."

"How could I forget them? You included them in every stack of paperwork for the last two weeks." Charles knew his deputy was only looking out for him, but his lines were going to come from his heart, not his mind.

When Ravae stepped out of the conference room to go over some last details, Charles had a moment to himself. He was sitting in the same seat a year ago at the staff meeting when Cliff was swinging on the vine fussing with the CFO over funding for the Virtual Vine project.

Although frustrated at the time, Charles now had to chuckle to himself at how funny that actually looked. Gregory had reminded him that it was okay to have fun in the workplace, even if it meant "doing a few backflips" as long as the job was being done.

That said, Charles tried to provide more direction and focus at the Wednesday staff meetings. He turned his gaze to the side of the conference room where he had installed a large board with the LISTEN acronym that Kayla had shared with him.

GREAT LEADERS "LISTEN"

- **L**earn from others
- **I**nstill pride of ownership
- **S**hare the center stage
- **T**eamwork is promoted
- **E**go is kept in check
- **N**ew ideas are created

Charles asked Kayla to facilitate a half-day training session for his senior staff in this same conference room about the importance of the LISTEN philosophy. She was a big hit, and the staff seemed to enjoy her easy-to-follow approach. More than once during a staff meeting, Cliff or one of the others would point back to the big board to reinforce an idea just shared.

As Charles leaned back in his chair, he picked up the program that was nearly worn by the times that Ravae had read it and folded it back again. Today was the day when South Forest, North Forest, and the Elephant Herd Land would officially form a new government entity called Tri-Forest County. A new county commissioner would be sworn in as part of the ceremony to be held in the amphitheater.

"Charles, we are ready. Andreas will meet us at the ceremony. His elephant taxi ride just left," Ravae said.

When he stepped into the reception area, Taylor was waiting for him in a dress made especially for the big event.

"Taylor, you look more beautiful today than the day I married you. You are still the prettiest chimp in South Forest."

Ravae nodded her approval and then reached behind Andreas' desk to hand Charles a bouquet of flowers.

"Hon," Charles said, "I cannot tell you how much I appreciate all of your support during this last year. Your patience and understanding has made this hectic time endurable. Please accept these flowers as a small token of my love for you."

Ravae felt a tear in her eye as her boss hugged his wife.

The three chimps stepped out of the office and headed toward the treetop shuttle service. When they arrived, Charles noticed that Nathan and Gabe were on the two-ape lifting crew. He smiled because both of them were wearing formal attire, including a coat and bow tie.

Gabe spoke first. "What do you think, Mr. Charles? We are wearing them in honor of the big day."

Taylor nodded affirmatively. "I have never seen two more handsome gorillas in all my life." She covered her heart with her hand.

"I agree, hon," Charles said. "But when are you two going to attend the ceremony? I thought our trio was the last to board."

"Yes, sir, you are the last group," said Nathan. "And right on time is our elephant taxi ride coming up now."

"Okay then." Charles clapped his hands together one time. "Hoist us up, and we will see you on the other side."

After the trio was hoisted to the top of the tree platform, Charles looked down at the two apes and their elephant taxi escort and waved at them that it was okay to depart. Charles knew how to handle the gondola lift without any assistance, and the three chimpanzees were soon riding over the tree line for the ten-minute journey.

While Ravae and Taylor sat in the front seats and chatted about the ceremony, Charles enjoyed the view from the backseat that he never tired of, the beautiful jungle forest and the surrounding landscape around them. Far off to the north, he could see the dust rise from a herd of zebras running in unison.

During times and views like this one, Charles often thought of Gregory. He remembered the first time that he met his brother ape. The only reason Charles encountered the massive gorilla was because Gregory liked to get up early in the morning and spend time with nature. *How fortunate for me that I had met Gregory*, he thought.

Charles was a changed chimp. Sure, being a CEO would mean encountering some difficulties, but he now fully enjoyed his career and life in general. On that fateful day that seemed like only yesterday, Gregory and the other gorillas like Gil and Kayla had taught Charles many lessons.

As he looked down over the magnificent forest, he realized how Gregory had instilled in him the importance of a leader seeing the big picture. Upon his return from his visit to North Forest a year ago, Charles promoted Ravae to the deputy position and Andreas as his new special assistant.

Ravae's attention to detail and organizational skills immediately relieved Charles of the management tasks that burdened him from being a visionary leader. Furthermore, Andreas provided a fresh perspective that Charles often leveraged. In a few years, Charles hoped that Ravae would become the CEO and Andreas her deputy. Gorilla and chimp working together at that level brought a smile to his face.

"Are you okay, dear? You seem awfully quiet back there." Taylor turned back to Charles.

"I am fine, hon."

The two lady chimps continued their conversation. Returning to his thoughts, Charles remembered how Dawson had successfully established the Self-Review Program with Gil as the sponsor ape. Once again, Gregory supported the request for Dawson to visit CHIMP Inc. to share the concept with the senior team. The program was especially useful for the Virtual Vine project that encountered a few glitches during the final implementation phase.

As much as Gregory had willingly shared with the chimp community, he was always quick to emphasize how much the gorillas had gained in return. The alpha ape often told the story of how Charles had come up with the idea of Dawson's assignment as the self-review manager in the first place. Gregory constantly reminded the gorillas that the chimpanzees and they were of the same great ape family. Different species perhaps, but great apes nevertheless.

The young apes still regaled about how Charles had pumped wood in the fitness center. The legend had soon grown that he had lifted nearly half of what Gregory could lift. Gregory never corrected the upstart apes. He was proud of his friend's accomplishments, both in the strength room and as a leader.

Charles respected Gregory's physical strength but admired his strength of character even more. Gregory's willingness to hold Gil accountable for his delay in completing the self-review questions had to be especially difficult because he and Gil were friends and had known each other for so long.

Once Charles had recommended Dawson's selection as the self-review manager, Gregory could have moved on, but he instead made it a teaching moment for Kayla and Hannah. As a result, they were better leaders for Gregory's "tough love" feedback.

At the same time, Gregory showed tremendous humility. He seemed uncomfortable when any attention was given to him. Charles remembered how Gregory chose to sit at the very back of the amphitheater with Gil at the performance instead of in the front row.

Above all, the alpha ape demonstrated compassion to those around him. Charles recalled how Gregory continuously addressed Dawson's accident and the impact on him and his gorilla family. Many bosses might have left those details to other managers to address, but Gregory stayed with it until reaching a good solution. Charles recognized that Gregory had been transformational when he recommended formally integrating the two communities and then proposed including the elephants as well. Yes, the alpha ape was a great leader, and he would be instrumental in the future of all communities.

As the gondola lift approached the other side, Charles noticed Cyrus waiting for the group. When the lift was properly secured, Cyrus opened up the side door to let the trio debark on the platform.

"Right on time," Cyrus proclaimed. "The amphitheater is overflowing today, and electricity is in the air. I know I speak for all of South Forest when I say how proud of you we are, Charles. Very proud indeed."

"Thank you, sir, and I appreciate your unwavering support as well." Charles looked down and noticed that Grover and Galileo made up the lifting crew. "My, how they have grown over the last year. They are almost as big as Dawson," Charles said to no one in particular.

When they made it down, the four began the short walk to the auditorium's southern entrance. Charles said he would meet them after the ceremony as he took his designated position, as practiced a few days earlier.

There was a loud ovation as Charles walked up the steps to the center of the stage. He noticed Cliff doing backflips on the northern wall of the amphitheater. When the applause did not die down as expected, he made a halting motion to the massive crowd to restore order.

"Thank you," Charles humbly replied. "Today is a special day as we form our Tri-County partnership and incorporation of South Forest, North Forest, and the Elephant Herd Land."

Again, there was a tremendous outpouring of cheers and applause, and it took the chimpanzee another minute to gain control.

"The selection of the first Tri-County commissioner is equally important as we have come together to choose a new leader that will provide the wisdom and vision for generations to come. At this time, it gives me great pleasure to introduce my brother ape, Gregory, to the stage."

As Gregory walked up the steps to the stage, Charles stepped toward him with his outstretched hand, knuckles facing outward. Gregory grazed the chimp's hand in like manner. The applause was as loud and long as the one given for Charles.

Gregory had prepared only a few words to say for this momentous occasion. He turned to his right to see Charles smiling with his arms folded in front of him. When the crowd quieted down, he said, "It is my honor … my great honor … to present to you the new Tri-County commissioner, my mentor and my friend, Edna."

With the announcement, a dozen elephants that were lined up next to the southern wall, raised their trunks, and trumpeted in a new leader and a new era of prosperity for the jungle community.

JUNGLE REFLECTIONS:
TESTING YOUR GQ

In the following discussion questions, we go back even deeper in the jungle. You are encouraged to read each discussion question and reflect for a moment before answering them. After every discussion question, a leadership tip is associated with each of the topics.

1. What were some of the issues frustrating Charles that led him to take his long walk to the North Forest in the first place? (Chapter One)

Leadership is not easy. Sometimes, the pressures of managing budgets, meeting deadlines, and leading others can make us feel isolated and aggravated. As a leader, we need to find alternative ways to refresh. Schedule a day off that does not involve a family vacation or a trip, that is, just some personal downtime. Take a stroll during the lunch hour, and get away from the office.

Gregory and Charles demonstrated the need for leaders to refresh in order to reengage. Gregory did so routinely by getting up early in the morning to spend time with nature and to reflect. Charles, of course, started his life-changing journey by walking on a trail by himself to contemplate on that fateful morning's events.

2. Identify the strengths and weaknesses of the CHIMP Inc. senior staff that reported to Charles. (Chapter Four)

_____

_____

_____

_____

_____

_____

_____

_____

_____

_____

_____

_____

_____

_____

_____

_____

_____

_____

_____

_____

_____

Diversity is more than just differences in what we can see. It can include diversity of thought. A leader needs to leverage individual differences and harvest them into team strength. How effective would Charles' staff meeting been if chimps were calm and in agreement about the issues in front of them?

Instead of shutting down the dialogue, a leader should encourage looking at a challenge from multiple angles. A spirited debate or even a good laugh can stimulate innovative juices. The right answer is good. The right question is even better.

3. After Gregory mixed it up with the younger apes in the work yard, Charles asked why he had disrupted the calm setting. What was Gregory's explanation for doing so? (Chapter Nine)

_____

_____

_____

_____

_____

_____

_____

_____

_____

_____

_____

_____

_____

_____

_____

_____

_____

_____

_____

_____

A leader needs to connect with the workforce on a regular basis. Gregory challenged the young gorillas to set a record during the next Tree Run through the Forest competition. If they beat it, he would wear his wife's pink dress at the awards ceremony.

Reassess how you connect with your staff. Do you meet personally with newcomers? Consider establishing all-hands meetings to share information, acknowledge top performers, and answer questions.

4. Gregory confronted Gil's apparent apathy toward the new Self-Review Program. Describe ways that Gregory held him accountable while demonstrating compassion at the same time. (Chapter Fourteen)

_____

_____

_____

_____

_____

_____

_____

_____

_____

_____

_____

_____

_____

_____

_____

_____

_____

_____

_____

_____

_____

Ultimately, a leader is first responsible to ensure mission accomplishment and, second, to encourage and develop employees. A leader is wise to keep emotions in check when confronting a situation when an employee falls short.

Gather all the facts before becoming extremely angry and doing even more damage. However, if the employee deserves to be held accountable after further review, then do so accordingly.

5. Explain why Kayla and Hannah felt their options for Dawson after his accident were the right ones. Describe why Gregory did not support their proposal and how he responded to both of them. (Chapter Fifteen)

_____

_____

_____

_____

_____

_____

_____

_____

_____

_____

_____

_____

_____

_____

_____

_____

_____

_____

_____

A leader should take inputs and recommendations and challenge assumptions if necessary. In the Dawson situation, Kayla and Hannah were too quick to propose a benefits or resource-driven solution. Gregory reminded them that AR is about the ape, not just job benefits.

Explain your own rationale and logic when making a different decision than the one recommended. Use these situations as a teaching moment.

6. Explain how both Gregory and Brayson (the personal trainer) had stereotyped Charles at the fitness center. Did Charles respond appropriately? (Chapter Sixteen)

_____

_____

_____

_____

_____

_____

_____

_____

_____

_____

_____

_____

_____

_____

_____

_____

_____

_____

_____

In order to be a complete or total leader, a leader must lead all those on the team, not just a select few. Are there situations where you are not maximizing individual contributions to the mission because of a negative stereotype?

A leader should create an environment where all can participate so all can contribute. Doing so will improve morale, teamwork, and professional development and ultimately help achieve the goals and objectives of the organization.

Additional Discussion Questions

- Did Gregory's announcement of Edna as the new Tri-Country commissioner surprise you? Why do you think she was the best choice for the important new position?
- Give examples of how Charles applied Gregory's APE advice when he returned to South Forest.
- What were some of Charles' personal characteristics that won over Gregory as a friend and brother ape?
- Explain how the death of Gregory's father and how he died affected Gregory's outlook and behavior.
- Describe the relationship between Gregory and Gil, the branch chief. What made it special or different?
- What led to a breakthrough between Gregory and Ryan, the union representative?
- Why did Gregory insist that Dawson work directly for Gil in his new role as the self-review program manager?
- What was the significance of Gregory sitting in the back of the amphitheater during the recital? Describe Charles' reaction to the alpha ape's decision.

ABOUT THE AUTHOR

J oseph Garcia is the vice president of finance/chief financial officer (CFO) for The Citadel, Military College of South Carolina located in Charleston. He is a colonel in the South Carolina Uniformed Militia. He was the first and only CFO for FEMA Hurricane Katrina Gulf Coast Recovery operations in their New Orleans, Louisiana, oversight office. He performed in this senior executive service position for three years. His mantra was "to not sacrifice the recovery mission, but to honor the sacrifices of the American taxpayers who entrusted us with their resources." Garcia led the development of the first ever budget for recovery operations and initiated a Good Stewardship Council for the entire Gulf Coast. The Department of Homeland Security awarded him a Superior Mission Achievement award.

His other CFO assignments were for a federal agency and a national nonprofit, both in Washington DC. On a volunteer basis, he is board chairman for another nonprofit that supports women and children who suffer from human rights abuses.

Joseph spent twenty-eight years on active duty in the United States Air Force, where he served as a squadron commander and spent a tour at the Pentagon. He was deployed for six months in the Middle East, and he served in numerous overseas assignments, including South Korea and Germany. While assigned to the Air Force Academy, he taught a leadership course to upper-division cadets in addition to being a training director and a regional director of admissions. He retired at the rank of lieutenant colonel. He holds an executive master's in leadership from Georgetown University in Washington DC and now teaches leadership classes at The Citadel. His other awards include the Federal Woman's Program Male Boss of the Year and Department of Defense Comptroller of the Year.

He and his wife, Brenda, reside in Charleston, South Carolina.

OTHER BOOKS BY THE AUTHOR

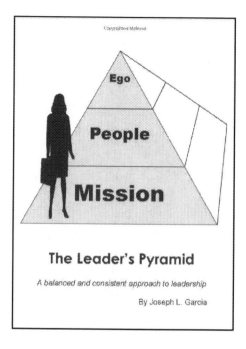